Internet Marketing for Plumbing & HVAC Contractors

How to TRIPLE Your Sales By Getting Your Internet Marketing Right

Joshua D. Nelson

Publisher: Clic Inc, 3401 NW 82 Ave #350, Doral, Florida 33122

While they have made every effort to verify the information here, neither the author nor the publisher assumes any responsibility for errors in, omissions from or different interpretation of the subject matter. This information may be subject to varying laws and practices in different areas, states and countries. The reader assumes all responsibility for use of the information.

The author and publisher shall in no event be held liable to any party for any damages arising directly or indirectly from any use of this material. Every effort has been made to accurately represent this product and its potential and there is no guarantee that you will earn any money using these techniques.

ISBN-13: 978-1502548740
ISBN-10: 1502548747

CONTENTS

ACKNOWLEDGMENTS

This book is based on real world case studies of Plumbing & HVAC companies across the country who have doubled, tripled and 10X'ed their sales by getting their internet marketing right.

I'd like to acknowledge our clients who allowed us to use their stories as the foundation for this book.

Special thanks to Mark Norman of Shamrock Plumbing, Tracy & Bill Bennett of The Plumbing Dr., Rich Hull of Hull Plumbing, Jeannie & Michael Petri of Petri Plumbing, Geno Caccia of James Caccia Plumbing, Greg Joyce of Schuler Services, Phillip Maurici of The Clean Plumbers, Matt Hord of The Plumbing Services Company, Michael & Sal De Florio of AAA Modern Air, Bethany McKeon of Jerry Kelly, Sam Garber of Samco Plumbing, Dan & Sam Dowdy of S&D Plumbing, Jim Wagner of Jim Wagner Plumbing, Vince Lambert of Lambert Plumbing & Heating, James Ferguson of Priced Right Heating & Cooling, Daniel Cordova of Daniel Cordova Plumbing, Ron Griesmer of Johnson Home Comfort, Scott Kissinger of The Plumbing Works and the countless other Plumbing & HVAC companies who lent their experience and story to the development of this book.

Joshua D. Nelson

INTRODUCTION

In this book, we are going to be talking about how you can triple your sales by getting your Internet marketing right in your plumbing or HVAC business.

I'm delighted you're reading because it's great to see how many people are interested in growing their business and leveraging the Internet to the fullest.

I am really excited about what I have to share here.

I want to emphasize that this book is based on case studies and real life examples.

This isn't me throwing out hype.

It's truly based on other companies

> Everything here is based on real world, in the trenches experience and stuff you can take to the bank.

we've been able to help double, triple and even in some cases 10x their sales.

It's good solid information that you can sink your teeth into and feel confident that, if implemented correctly, will have an impact on the growth of your company.

Have You Ever Wondered?

I will start by asking, have you ever wondered what it would be like:

- To have a dominant presence that positioned you as the top plumbing or HVAC business in your area?
- To have a flood of prospects calling in to your business on a consistent basis that found you online?
- To know that you were leveraging the Internet to its fullest, in terms of exposure, leads, and profits?

That's really what I want for you through this book.

What You'll Find in This Book

As you read this book, you're about to discover:

- A blueprint covering the most important online marketing media that you should be tapping into for your plumbing or HVAC business.
- How you can get your plumbing or HVAC company ranked on Page One for the most important key words for your area.
- A proven strategy for getting ranked on the Google Map listings in your market.
- Our step-by-step strategy for getting more repeat and referral business by leveraging social media.

Again, it's all based on real world examples and case studies of other plumbing and HVAC companies just like yours.

In some of the most important areas, I've provided quite a bit of step-by-step detail and have separated it out into a Special Briefing section.

Who Am I?

Before we get too deep, I'd like to introduce myself. So who am I, and why should you listen?

My name is Josh Nelson. I'm the CEO of Plumbing and HVAC SEO.

I'm the author of "The Complete Guide to Internet Marketing for Plumbing Contractors," which is available on Amazon.com. I'm an Associate Member of PHCC, QSC, and ACCA.

I've had the opportunity to speak at a number of the PHCC, QSC and other industry events, both on the national and local level.

A number of my articles on Internet marketing have been published in "Plumbing and Mechanical Contractor Magazine," "Contractor Magazine" and "HVAC Insider."

I'm widely accepted as the premier expert in Internet marketing for plumbing and HVAC businesses.

But really, I think more important than any of that stuff, I've had the opportunity to work hands on with literally hundreds of plumbing and HVAC companies all throughout the United States and internationally.

I have been able to help them go from virtually no placement online to the point where they're now the dominant player in their market.

A lot of them have doubled, tripled, and in some cases 10x their sales by getting their Internet marketing right.

So, everything I'm going to be bringing to you from a training perspective is based on real world, in the trenches experience and stuff you can take to the bank.

What We Do

Spoiler alert, our company does this stuff. We specialize in working with plumbing and HVAC companies and managing their Internet marketing strategy.

We will set up your website, ensure that you're optimized for the search engines, write your content, manage your blog, update your social media profiles, develop your authority via citation development, link building and review management, track your online rankings and ROI putting the strategies outlined in this book into action and implementing them for you.

Our team is based in Doral, Florida. It's a real brick and mortar company with writers, account managers, link builders, web designers, and graphic designers.

Working with You

Obviously, we'd love the opportunity to work with you and do this for you.

But that's not what the purpose of this book is; this isn't going to be a veiled sales presentation.

I really want to give you our best knowledge and information on how to proactively market your plumbing or HVAC business on your own.

If you were to take this information and implement it, I'd want you to be able to take it and succeed with it.

That's what we're doing in this book, it's not a sales presentation.

Yes, we'd love to work with you, we'd love to have you as a client but that's not what this book is all about.

Josh Nelson

WHY THE INTERNET MATTERS:
A TRUE LIFE STORY

Let's get into the nitty-gritty. How can you triple your sales by getting your Internet marketing right?

As I said in the introduction, this entire book is based on case studies and real world examples.

So the first case study I'm going to talk about is The Plumbing Doctor.

The Plumbing Doctor is based in Falls Church, Virginia. They've been in business for about 25 years, it's a two generation company owned by Dr. Bill and his daughter Tracy.

They built their business over the years by advertising heavily in the Yellow Pages.

The Decline of Yellow Pages

In their market, in and around Falls Church / Arlington, Virginia, they had the double truck ad and they were aggressive advertisers in their local Yellow Pages.

They built a very significant, very profitable plumbing business in their market. Now somewhere along the way – around the mid-2000s – they noticed a decline.

They noticed that the Yellow Pages weren't driving the same number of calls, the same number of leads that they once did.

So the owner Dr. Bill – as he refers to himself – decided:

"Man we really need to figure out where the customers have shifted. If they're not going to the Yellow Pages, they have to be going somewhere. We have to figure out where they are going, so we can tap into and make sure our business doesn't go by the wayside."

He realized – like you probably did – that there was that transition from offline to online. It shifted so that the predominant place that people looked when they needed plumbing and HVAC services moved from the Yellow Pages to the Internet.

He realized that nowadays when someone needs a plumber or needs HVAC repair, they are going to the Internet.

Statistics tell us that 97 percent of consumers are going to the web when they're looking for these plumbing and HVAC related services.

With that in mind, he decided, "We've got to get aggressive with Internet marketing, we have to put a strategy in place and tap into this opportunity."

First Foray into Internet Marketing – Yellow Pages

So, since the Yellow Pages had treated him so well over the years and he did build a good base of business from it, the first thing he did was speak to the Yellow Pages rep.

The rep came in and said, "Hey, we shifted too, now we're online. We'll setup your website and we will get you on the Internet."

So it seemed like a no-brainer and that's what he decided to do. He signed up with Yellow Pages and they put together a website for him; they got some online placement in YP.com. But it fell flat for him.

- He didn't get a lot of return of investment.
- He didn't get a lot of calls.

Part of the problem with his strategy was that, while Yellow Pages did set up a website for him and they did get him on YP.com, he wasn't showing up on Google, Yahoo, and Bing.

These are the three major places that people search for plumbing & HVAC services. In addition, his website wasn't compelling.

- They gave him a cookie cutter website
- It didn't have any personality
- It didn't differentiate him from the competition

It was clear this wasn't going to work.

Trying the Pay-per-click Option

So his next path was to try pay-per-click advertising. What happened at this time was one of the big pay-per-click management companies like ReachLocal or Yodle came in; they had a nice presentation and showed him some great call tracking and tracking technology.

They said, "We're going to put an aggressive pay-per-click marketing strategy in place for you and your phone is going to ring off the hook."

Well, this strategy did have a little bit of an impact.

> 80 percent of consumers searching on Google, Yahoo or Bing for plumbing or HVAC related services are looking at the non-paid listings (Map and organic) listings.

Now he was showing up on Google, he was getting more people to his website.

However, it fell a little bit flat, no matter how much he spent – and the budget that they recommended was between $1,500 and $3,000 per month – it felt like he only barely broke even.

If he spent $1,500 then he only made enough to cover that. It certainly wasn't replacing the profitability and the volume of calls that he was getting in the heyday, when he was the big guy in the Yellow Pages.

The problem with this strategy was yes he was showing up in the paid listings, but he wasn't showing up in the organic listings.

Statistics tell us that more than 80 percent of consumers when they're searching on Google or they are searching on Yahoo or Bing looking for plumbing or HVAC related services, are looking at the Map listings, they're looking at the organic listings, they're looking at the non-paid listings.

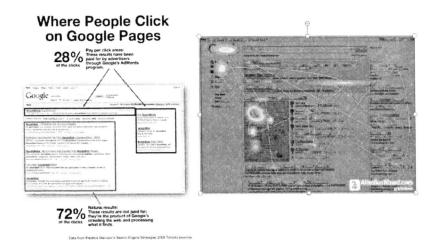

He was missing almost 80 percent of the traffic with this strategy.

The other big problem with this strategy was he was still working off a basic template website that didn't have any unique personality, didn't have any unique branding, didn't separate him from the competition.

Back to the Drawing Board

Again, he was back to the drawing board thinking, "What am I going to do in order to get past this hump so I can continue to grow my business?"

We were able to come in and help him get his online marketing right.

In this book, I am going to be breaking down the strategy and the things that we implemented that you can model in your business.

- We got into the website and we updated it, so it had a little bit more of a web 2.0 design (as shown above).
- We made sure the site had personality, pictures of the owner, pictures of the staff.
- It had specific messaging why somebody would want to choose them versus the competition.
- It was optimized for the search engines. It had pages for every one of their services. It had pages for every one of the cities they operated in.
- It had good quality inbound links.
- They had online reviews.

What happened was, as that strategy was implemented, they started to show up in the place people were looking when people needed their services.

They started showing up when we typed in: "Falls Church Plumber," "Falls Church Plumbing," and "Falls Church Emergency Plumber."

In the illustration that follows, I've got some arrows pointing to the dominant positioning they were able to obtain. But here's really what I want you to see – the result of this:

- Prior to implementing this and getting the online marketing right, they were averaging about 254 visitors to the website each month.
- A little bit less than four months after getting the organic side of the equation right so that the website started ranking well organically and converting better, that number jumped – as you can see in the following chart – from 254 visitors to 733 visitors.

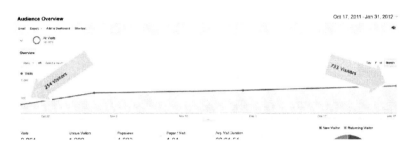

What's instructive here is that they went from 24 calls to 88 calls directly from the Internet.

In their case, that's a three times increase in calls, in leads and in revenues that they were extracting from the Internet as a company.

So what this meant for them was they were able to keep the staff that they had without feeling that they needed to downsize.

And Dr. Bill was able to feel confident that he had a growing, sustainable business that he can someday hand down to his daughter, Tracy.

What does this mean for you? Well let's break it down step-by-step.

CREATING AN ACTION PLAN FOR YOUR OWN SUCCESS

Now that we've talked about a real life example, let's dive in to the strategy and I'll show you how you can create an action plan to apply this in your own plumbing or HVAC business.

I'll start with an overview of the strategy we followed for that case study example.

Then I'll go into detail on some of the key elements so that you can apply them in your own business.

First of all, it's important to recognize there are two keys to success with your website:

- **SEO**, which is making sure that your site is optimized to show up in your organic listing when someone types in the key words that are important to you.
- **Conversion** is probably just as important and that is what is it about your website that resonates with the customer that's looking for your services, so that they pick up the phone and call you as opposed to hitting the back button and searching around.

In addition, it's important to ensure your website is mobile ready.

Key Strategies

The following are some of the strategies we used in the case study example.

We got very active with link building to develop authority. I'm going to talk about of some of the right link building strategies and the right way to do these versus the wrong way.

We also made sure the site was optimized correctly for the Google Map listings, by making sure there was consistency of their name, address and phone number.

We put an aggressive review automation process in place, to get reviews from real customers in the true service area.

This was backed up by an aggressive social media campaign on Facebook, Twitter, Google+ and LinkedIn – together with a YouTube channel and interesting videos.

We leveraged email marketing by collecting emails and pushing out a newsletter on a consistent basis.

Then we looked at and implemented some paid online marketing channels and you saw the numbers that I just mentioned.

That three times increase I mentioned was only based on organic results – getting ranked in the non-paid listings.

> We had the right tracking and measurements in place, so we knew when the website traffic and call volume increased.

These numbers went up significantly when we started to implement pay-per-click advertising, paid ads on Angie's List and some of the other channels.

The other critical and unspoken piece of the equation was making sure we had the right tracking and measurements in place, so we knew when the traffic to the website and call volume increased.

We were looking for increased ranking as well as increased traffic to the website.

So at a high level, that was the strategy we followed.

Creating Your Action Plan

Now let's shift into implementation mode and let's create an action plan to implement this in your business so that you can get similar results.

To help you through this process, I'd encourage you to download a worksheet that I've posted online.

You can download this worksheet at
http://www.plumberseo.net/handout

It features a set of questions and I'll actually be following these questions for the rest of this book.

I want you to be able to finish this book with a plan of action; I don't want you just to absorb all the information and do nothing.

> I want you to be able to finish this book with a plan of action.

I want you to think about:

- How does this apply to my business?
- What do I need to do if I want to double or triple or 10x my sales?

I can't think of a better way to do that than to work through a worksheet and the questions together and come up with a plan of action as a result.

There is also a copy of this worksheet at the back of the book, but as I stated earlier, you can also download a copy at:

www.plumberseo.net/handout

I'd recommend that you download a copy of the worksheet so we can go through this together and create your action plan.

#1: Do You Have a Website?

The first question is do you have a website?

As you're reading this book, I imagine that you already have a website and you're trying to figure out how to get your online marketing strategy right.

If you don't yet have a website, definitely circle that on the worksheet.

That's something you can take action on right away.

But, assuming you do have a website, put a little check next to that one and pat yourself on the back because that's the first step.

You have to have a website if you're going to be active in Internet marketing for your plumbing or HVAC company.

#2: Does Your Website Show Up in Search?

The next question is a little bit more pointed and that's, "Does your website show up in search?"

So is it showing up when someone goes onto Google.com and types in the keywords that are important to your company – that might be "your city plumber", "your city plumbing", "your city ac repair", "your city heating contractor"?

In order to answer that question you need to understand what I'm talking about and we need to do a little brainstorming on the keywords that are important in your business.

But, before we dive too deep into that specific topic, I want to make sure you're clear on the difference between:

- Paid listings (PPC)
- Map listings
- Organic listings

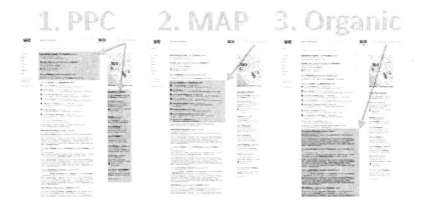

1. **Paid/PPC Listings** – In the paid section of the search engines, you are able to select the keywords that are relevant to you and then pay to be listed in this area. The reason it is referred to as PPC – or Pay-Per-Click – is because you pay each time someone clicks on your link rather than paying a flat monthly or daily fee for placement.

2. **Map Listings** – The Map listings have become very important because it is the first thing that comes up in the search results for most locally based searches. If someone searches "AC Repair + your city", chances are the Map listings will be the first thing they look at. Unlike the paid section of the search engine, you can't buy your way into the Map listings. You have to earn it. Once you do, there is no per-click cost associated with being in this section of the search engine.

3. **Organic Listings** – The organic/natural section of the search engine results page appears directly beneath the Map listings in many local searches, but appears directly beneath the paid listings in the absence of the Map listings (the Map section only shows up in specific local searches). Similar to the Map listings, you can't pay your way into this section of the search engines and there is no per-click cost associated with it.

When it comes to the question, "How am I ranking in search?" I'm more interested in whether you are showing up on the Map and in the organic listings.

Are you showing up in those non-paid listings, where the majority of traffic goes?

I mentioned earlier that more than 80 percent of consumers, when they're searching, their eyeballs ignore the paid listings and go straight to the Map and organic listings.

Choosing Keywords

So what keywords are you or are you not ranking for?

It's easy to say "I show up for my company name".

But that's not very relevant, that's not going to help you drive more calls and more leads.

Really, you have to think through what people are typing in when they need your services.

In the Appendix at the back of this book, I've given you an example list of the most commonly searched keywords for plumbing and another one for HVAC. You can download a list of the most commonly searched plumbing & HVAC keywords by going to the links, below:

www.plumberseo.net/plumbing-keywords

www.hvacseo.net/keywords

So, on the plumbing side, they're going to type out a lot of things and the obvious ones are:

- "Your city" plumber
- "Your city" plumbing
- "Your city" plumbing services

The less than obvious examples are things like:

- Water heater installation
- Water heater repair
- Bathroom remodeling
- Trenchless sewer replacement
- Sump pump installation
- Gas line installation and repair

There's a lot of a different things that you do as a company, so in this first question that I'm asking, you really need to think through, are you showing up in the organic listings for what you do?

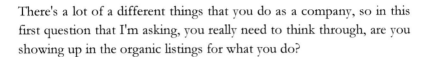

ACTION STEP: I want you to map out a list of the top ten keywords that you think people are typing when they need your services. You can learn more about this concept by going to http://www.plumberseo.net/plumbing-keywords

The list I have given you at the end of the book is based on our research on what we know people are typing in.

Then start to look on Google, Yahoo and Bing and see if you are ranking on the Map and the organic listings for these keywords.

If you're not, I'm going to be showing you how to get ranked, but you want to make sure that you start to put a strategy in place to show up in that area.

On the HVAC side, look at the air conditioning and heating related keywords. It's going to be:

- "Your city" air conditioning
- Air conditioner
- AC installation
- AC repair
- Heater repair
- Furnace repair
- HVAC contractor

Again, the same concept rings true. Start to develop your list of keywords and test yourself and find out where you rank currently.

If you're not aware whether you're ranking well or not, you might not realize there's something that needs to be fixed.

Start there, that's the first step.

Are you showing up organically for the keywords that people are typing in when they need your services?

#3: Is Your Website Properly Optimized for Search?

The next question on our list is, is your website properly optimized?

There's no way it's going to show up in the search engines if it's not optimized in a way that Google understands what pages, what keywords it should be showing up for.

> Your website is only going to show up in the search engines if it's optimized in a way that Google understands what pages, what keywords it should be showing up for.

Let me give you a crash course in optimizing your website, or at least looking at your website and telling whether it's optimized or not.

Getting your plumbing or HVAC company listed in the organic (non-paid listings) section of the search engines comes down to two core factors:

- It is important to have the proper on-page optimization so that Google knows what you do and the area you serve, so that it can put it in the index for the right keywords. You do this by having pages for each of your services and then optimizing them for specific keyword combinations (Ex. your city + main service, your city + service 2, your city + service 3, etc.)

- You must create enough authority and transparency so that Google ranks you on page one (rather than page ten) for those specific keywords. Ultimately, it comes down to having credible inbound links and citations from other websites to your website. He who has the most credible inbound links, citations and reviews, wins.

How to Map Out the Pages that Should be Included on Your Website for Maximum Results

In the previous chapter, I asked you to spend some time thinking about your most important keywords in your area, you can start to map out the pages that you should add to your website.

Keep in mind that each page on your website can only be optimized for 1-2 keyword combinations.

If you came up with 25 keywords then you are going to need at least 12 – 15 pages on your website.

You need to be sure you have each keyword mapped to a specific page on your site.

Keyword	Mapped to what page
Main Keyword	Home
Keyword 1	Services – Keyword 1
Keyword 2	Services – Keyword 2
Keyword 3	Services – Keyword 3
Keyword 4	Services – Keyword 4
Keyword 5	Services – Keyword 5

So, for your plumbing company you might come up with the following keywords:

Plumber, Plumbing, Emergency Plumber, Drain Cleaning, Water Heater Repair

Keyword	Mapped to what page
City Plumber	Home Page
City Plumbing Contractor	Home Page
City Emergency Plumber	Emergency Plumber Page
City Drain Cleaning	Drain Cleaning Page
City Water Heater Repair	City Water Heater Repair
City Roofing Contractor	City 2 Roofing Page

Now that you have mapped out the pages that need to be added to your website, you can start to think about how to optimize each of those pages for the search engines (Google, Yahoo and Bing).

using this pg

review Ray monte website.

How to Optimize Your Website and Pages for Ranking in the Organic Listings on Major Search Engines

Step 1 – Build out the website and obtain more placeholders on the major search engines.

A typical plumbing or HVAC website has only five to six pages (Home – About Us – Our Services – Coupons – Contact Us). That does not create a lot of indexation or placeholders on the major search engines.

Most Plumbing and HVAC contractors provide a wide variety of services.

By building out the website and creating separate pages for each of

> By building out the website and creating separate pages for each service, you can get listed on the search engines for each of the different keyword combinations.

these services (combined with city modifiers), you can get listed on the search engines for each of those different keyword combinations.

Here is an example:

- Home – About – Services - Coupons – Contact Us

- Sub-pages for each service – Miami Emergency Plumber, Miami Leak Detection, Miami Toilet Repair, Miami Water Heater Installation, Miami Tankless Water Heater, etc.

Many contractors provide services to a large number of cities outside of the city in which the business resides. In order to be found on the major search engines for EACH of those sub-cities, you need to create additional pages:

- Sub-pages for each sub-city serviced – Kendall Plumber, Doral Plumber, Homestead Plumber, etc.

Step 2 – Optimize Pages for Search Engines

Once the pages are built for each of your core services and sub-pages, each of the pages need to be optimized from an SEO perspective so that the search engines understand what the page is about and list you for those words.

Here are some of the most important items that need to be taken care of for on-page search engine optimization:

- Unique title tag on each page

- H1 tag restating that title tag on each page

- Images named with primary keywords

- URL should contain page keyword

- XML sitemap should be created and submitted to Google Webmaster Tools and Bing Webmaster Tools

Optimizing Title Tags

Many people make the mistake of having title tags that don't help get better search engine results.

For example, they may just have the name of their business.

Optimized Title Tag

Typical Plumbing Site Title

• Joe's Plumbing

SEO Optimized Title Tag

• Orlando Plumber | Shamrock Plumbing Orlando, FL | Orlando Repipe

For best results, you want a title tag that is optimized for the appropriate keywords.

H1 Tags

Another important way to ensure the best search results is to ensure the main heading – the H1 tag – repeats the desired keywords.

Different Services and Locations

Again, you want to make sure that you have your different keywords for the different services you provide on the different pages of your site. You want to have your keywords in those areas.

> In addition to keyword optimization, your content has to be good.

It's important to note, with the latest changes in the Google algorithm, your content has to be good, in addition to keyword optimization.

- It has to be compelling.
- It has to answer questions.

Great content is key.

Again, if you want to rank for hydro-jetting or trenchless sewer replacement, you need a specific page for that on your website. That page, of course has the proper title tag, H1 tag and great content for that specific topic.

The other thing we find with plumbing and HVAC companies is that most serve between a 25 and 50 mile radius.

Within that 25 to 50 mile radius, there's a lot of little sub-cities and sub-towns. If you want to rank for those sub-cities in your area – McLean, Fairfax and Vienna or whatever – you need to have a specific page for each one of those.

Of course, the same optimization principles ring true. So make sure that each sub-city page has a good title tag with your keyword in it, along with a good H1 tag and unique content.

This is something I want to really emphasize. The algorithm is constantly changing.

It used to be, for all your sub-city pages, you could just go ahead and change the city and have everything else be the same. However, that's not effective anymore.

You need to make sure that you're rewriting unique content for each and every single one of your cities, if you want to wind up potentially ranking well in those markets.

So that's really the question of, is your site properly optimized?

The things you want to look at are:

- Do you have your keywords in the title tag?
- Do you have pages for each one of your services?
- Do you have pages for each one of the brands that you serve?

- Do you have unique content on your website, on every single page as opposed to leveraging duplicate content?
- Do you have pages for each one of your sub-markets that you operate in?

This little piece right here is huge. If you can't check these items off on your worksheet, I would circle them on the worksheet, and I would say, "OK, I need to either get with my team, get with an outside provider or get with somebody that could help me set this up correctly so I can get into Google's index for the keywords and the services that I provide."

#3: Is Your Website Optimized for Conversion?

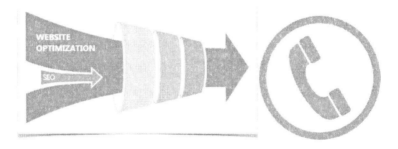

Moving forward, the next question is, is your website optimized for conversion?

Now you may think that, as an SEO or Internet marketing guy, the tendency would be that I wouldn't care so much about conversion, that all I care about is getting the website ranked in search. However, that's a recipe for failure.

You can have the number one listing and you can get hundreds of qualified visitors to your website on a daily basis – but, if the website's not compelling, if you don't give specific reasons for someone to contact you versus the competition, you might not get any calls.

If you're not getting any calls, or you're not getting as many calls as you could, then you're leaving money on the table.

It's real important that you don't just optimize for search, but you also optimize for conversion. By that I mean conversion from visitor to caller. Here are some of the best practices we've found to really improve the conversion rate on your website.

> **Have your phone number in the header graphic on your website.**

Have it in big bold letters: "Call now, anytime, to schedule an appointment". Just having that on every page of your website is best practice.

> **Have a web form where they can enter their name, phone number, email address and a brief description of their problem.**

Have that in the sidebar, somewhere on every page of your website, so you make it real easy for your potential customer to reach out to you and request contact.

> ➤ **One that might not be quite as obvious is to leverage personality.**

I see so many plumbing and HVAC websites that all they use is stock photography.

There's the real pretty family, there's the generic guy with the wrench in his hand, and it's not compelling at all.

> The more authentic your website is, the higher probability that it's going to convert well from visitor to caller.

It doesn't resonate with that potential customer. We've tested this, we've split tested this, on companies that have generic versus authentic imagery, and authentic imagery wins every single time.

Use real pictures of the owner, real pictures of the team, real pictures of the office, real pictures of the truck. The more authentic your website is, the more real it is, the better it resonates, and the higher probability that it's going to convert well from visitor to caller.

> **Leverage your credibility symbols.**

When people get to your website, they don't know who to trust, they're unsure.

They've got 100 different websites that they can look at when choosing a plumbing or HVAC company.

Give them some of the things they know and trust.

If you're an Angie's List Super Service

award recipient, go ahead and put that on your website.

If you're a member of the BBB, if you're a member of the local chamber of commerce, showcase that stuff, and try and showcase it above the fold.

Even if they don't spend any time clicking on it, they see it subliminally, it makes them feel more comfortable calling you and doing business with you.

> **Showcase your online reviews and testimonials.**

Nothing is going to improve your conversion more than having real reviews from real customers in your true service area.

The arrow below on The Plumbing Doctor website points to a little badge that shows 145 reviews.

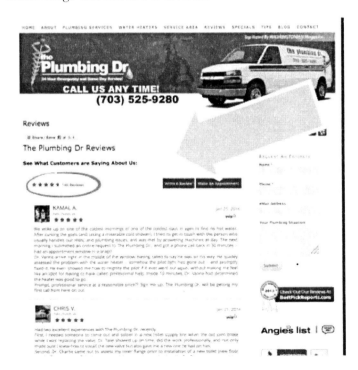

If you click that, it takes you to the reviews section on their website, where all of their reviews from across the web are showcased.

The way this works is the tool pulls their reviews. If they have 15 reviews on Yelp, 17 reviews on Angie's List, 33 reviews on the Google Map, it pulls them and aggregates them, and updates every time they get a four star review or higher.

Their website is really good at showcasing the good news, which makes it easy for people to call them and use them as opposed to the competition.

The lesson here is make sure that you're showcasing those positive reviews. So make sure you put some type of process in place to get online reviews from your real customers in your true service area.

On this issue of conversion, is your website optimized for conversion?

- Do you have the phone number in the top right hand corner of every page of your website?
- Are you using authentic imagery and videos?
- Do you tell a compelling story?
- Is there a reason that they would want to contact you versus the competition?

#4: Is Your Website Mobile Friendly?

Another really critical element of conversion is mobile. You've got to make sure that your website is mobile-friendly.

We know that there's 4.8 billion people that now own mobile phones.

Statistics tell us that three out of five consumers search for local businesses from their smart phone.

When somebody's got that plumbing problem, or

the AC's not working, more times than not, they're pulling out their mobile phone, and they're searching right there because it's more convenient.

They feel like it's an urgent situation to be resolved. If you don't have a good mobile experience – where they can browse up, down and simply press a button to call your office as in the example above – you could be losing traffic.

A report by Google shows that 40 percent of mobile consumers turn to a competitor's website after a bad mobile experience.

I would say if you don't have a mobile version of your website, you could be bleeding traffic. You could be sending your potential customers to the competition.

ACTION STEP: If you know your website is not mobile-friendly, or think it might not be, I would circle it on the worksheet and put a star next to it.

I wouldn't let this week go by without figuring out a solution to get a mobile-optimized version of your website. This isn't expensive, it's not hard to do, but don't let that one ride. Take some action on it immediately.

Just to answer one question I'm often asked, there is a difference between mobile-friendly versus mobile-responsive.

- **Mobile-friendly** would mean that someone goes to your website and it redirects to a mobile-optimized version of the site.
- **Mobile-responsive** is a site that's built specifically for all devices. Whether you got to it from your desktop or you got to it from a mobile phone, it's the same site, it shifts to fit the screen.

Latest best practices would tell us that a mobile-responsive website is better. We're moving towards that direction for all our clients.

#5: Are You Consistently Creating New Links, Content & Authority for Your Website?

The next piece of the equation is building inbound links and authority. To this point, we've talked about setting up your website:

- Optimizing it for the search engines by having pages for each one of your services and pages for each one of your cities.
- Making sure that you've got your title tags and your H1 tags right.
- Creating good content for each one of those pages and not having any duplicate content.

The next piece of the equation, then, is to build inbound links and authority.

You can have every page you need on your website – including a page for hydro-jetting and a page for drain cleaning – but that doesn't necessarily mean that you're ranking on page one for those keywords.

> What determines whether you're on page one is how Google deems the authority of that page.

That simply means that you've got a placeholder somewhere on Google for that keyword.

The thing that's going to determine whether you're on page one, or page 12, is really how Google deems the authority of that page in comparison to other pages on a similar topic.

All other things being equal, your authority is driven by the relevancy and the quality and quantity of good quality links back to your website.

I don't want this to get misconstrued. I don't want you to go out and build a bunch of random bad links.

As a matter of fact, the two most recent changes in the latest Google algorithm has been set up so that if you've got links to your website that aren't relevant, Google's actually penalizing you for that as opposed to promoting your website higher in the search engines.

Yes I want you to be strategic, I want you to build inbound links, because it does pass authority signals back to Google. However, if you've noticed a recent drop in your rankings, maybe in the last six to nine months, that's probably a result of bad links to your website.

There needs to be some type of thought process looking at your links, getting the bad ones either removed or disavowed, to really get things back on course.

Either way, you still need to be creating relevancy and building inbound links to your website.

Things to consider:

- Do you have somebody on your team that's managing this?
- Do you have somebody looking to see if you've got bad links?
- Do you have somebody proactively building relevant, quality inbound links to your website?
- Is there somebody responsible for updating your blog, or updating the content on your website on a consistent basis?

In the absence of that, your website's going to sit where it's at, without really progressing.

You have to have a strategy where you're consistently building that authority and building those links.

Because this is such an important area, I've covered this in more detail in a Special Briefing starting on the next page.

SPECIAL BRIEFING: BUILDING AUTHORITY

In this Special Briefing, we're going to look at how to build up the authority of your website so that you can rank on page one for your most important keywords.

Once the pages are built out and the "on-page" SEO is complete, the next step is getting inbound links. Everything we have done to this point is sort of like laying the ground work; you have to have the pages in order to be in the running.

But it is the number of QUALITY inbound links and web reference to those pages that is going to determine placement.

30% of SEO is On-Page type work. The other 70% is Authority Development, Citation Development & Link Building

Building out the pages is just the beginning. The only way to get your site to rank above your competition is by having MORE quality inbound links and citations to your site.

He Who Has The MOST Quality Inbound Links, WINS!

If there's any secret sauce to ranking well in the search engines, it is authority.

The major caveat however, is that you can't just create garbage links. You don't want to just have a thousand links. When I say links, I'm talking about other websites hyperlinking to your website.

The latest algorithm changes involve Google Panda and Google Penguin. Google is trying to prevent spam. A lot of internet marketers and SEO specialists realize it's all about the links. That's what the Google algorithm was built upon. They figured out ways to just get a bunch of links with random anchor text pointed back to the pages that they want to have ranked.

Those links weren't relevant and were from websites that really don't add any value to the Internet, and Google has recognized that. If you have bad or irrelevant links it can actually hurt your ranking more than help it. It's about getting quality relevant links back to your home page and sub-pages, through content creation and really strategic link building that will help you outrank your competition. How do you get these links? Where do you get these links?

Take a look at the visual below as a reference point. I call this my circle of linking opportunities:

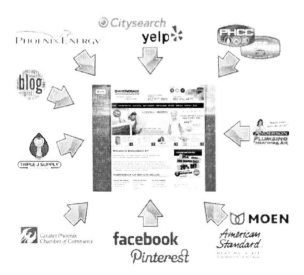

1. **Association Links:** Be sure that you have a link to your site from any industry associations that you belong to (Plumbing Association, Chamber of Commerce, Networking Groups, etc.).
2. **Directory Listings:** Get your site listed on as many directory type listings as possible (Angie's List, Yahoo Local Directory, Judy's Book, Yelp.com, etc.).
3. **Create interesting content/articles about your industry:** This is probably the #1 source of inbound links because you can write an article and push it out to thousands of article directory sites each containing a link back to a specific page on your site.
4. **Competitive Link Acquisition:** This is the process of using tools like Raven Tools, SEO Book and others to see what links your top competitors have, and then get those same or similar links pointed back to your website.

Let's look at each of these in more detail.

Directory Links

There's a number of what I like to call "low-hanging fruit," links. It all starts with your online directory listings.

Some examples include Google Maps, Yahoo Local, City Search, Yelp.com, Judy's Book, Best of the Web, Yellow Pages, Hot Frog, eLocal Plumber, Service Magic, and the list goes on.

All of these online listings let you list your company name, address, phone number and a link back to your website. Some of them even allow reviews.

For the most part, you can have yourself added to those directories completely free of charge, entering your company's name, address, phone number, description, and of course, a link back to your website.

They create some authoritative links back to your company. You want to make sure that you have your company listed on those online directory listings.

They're also valuable from a Google Maps optimization perspective because they give you citations, which are very important for getting ranked on the Map.

A great way to find additional online directories to add your company to would be to run a search on Google for "your company type – business directory," or "your city – business directory". This will give you a great list of potential directory sites that you can use to add your company.

There are also tools for this such as BrightLocal or White Spark that will provide you with a list of directory sources based on your industry. That's where you want to start, your online directory listings. From there, you want to look at any associations that you're involved with.

Association Links

In the visual, I reference PHCC and QSC. I'm assuming you are involved in some type of association, whether it is the national industry association, the local chapter or some other group affiliation. Visit the websites of those organizations and get listed in the member section. This will give you citations and the opportunity to link back to your website.

Affiliated Industries and Local Businesses that are Non-competitive

You can work with colleagues that have affiliated industry type businesses. If you're in plumbing, go to the HVAC contractors in your area and ask if they will post a link to your website on their own site and vice versa. Utilizing your resources and teaming up with relevant companies will add more authority to your domain.

Supplier Sites

The next thing you could look at is the suppliers that you purchase from. If you are a regular customer at American Standard, Moen or if you've got a co-op agreement with Bryant or some other manufacturer, try to coordinate a deal with them.

Oftentimes, the places where you buy your merchandise will have a section on their website that mentions their value add resellers. You can get a link from those.

Social Media Profile Links

The other "low hanging fruit" links are social media profiles. We have a whole section about the power of social media and how you can harness it to get repeat and referral business.

Simply from a link building perspective, you should set up a Facebook page, Twitter account, LinkedIn profile, Google Plus page, Pinterest profile and a YouTube channel and place a link to your website on each. Each one of them will allow you to enter your company's name, address, phone number, a description and, of course, a place to put your website address.

Local Associations

Other local associations that you're involved in – if you're a member of the Chamber of Commerce, a networking group like BNI (Business Networking International), or if you're involved with a local charity, find out if they list their members on their websites. Another great place to get links is by typing in 'your city + directory.'

Competitive Link Acquisition

You might be surprised that, if you really tackle these elements and you don't do any of the other things we have discussed, you will notice that you've probably got enough links to outrank your competition in your area.

> If you really tackle these elements, you will probably get enough links to outrank your competition.

I want to share some additional thoughts and strategies on how you can accomplish even more from a link building perspective.

A very powerful strategy that you can implement is called Competitive Link Acquisition.

The way I like to think of it is that if quality inbound links are the secret sauce to outranking your competition, and if we could figure out who's linking to your competition or what links your competition have, and we can get those same or similar links pointed back to your website, then you can outrank them, because you'll at that point have more authority.

Competitive link acquisition is the process of figuring out who is in the top position for your most important keywords, reverse engineering their link profile to see what links they have, and getting those same or similar links pointed back to your website.

A simple way to do this is just to go to Google.com and type in "your city + your service," and find out who is in the top few positions. Let's take a look at the number one placeholder.

He's there because his website is optimized well and Google knows that he should be ranked well based on the quality and quantity of inbound links compared to the competition.

Once you know who he is, you can use a couple of different tools such as Raven Tools, Majestic SEO, Back Link Watch, etc., and you can take their URL, input it into your tool of choice, run the report, and get a list of links in return.

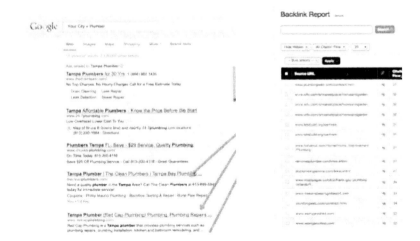

So, your number one competitor is "competitor1.com" for example. The link research tool spits out a list showing that they have 392 inbound links.

- They've got a link from the local Chamber of Commerce.
- They've got a link from the PHCC.
- They've got a link from an article that they posted in the local newspaper.
- They've got a link from the local networking chapter.

By analyzing the types of links that they have, you can systematically mimic those links and get them pointed back to your website.

Don't just do this for your first competitor, but also for your second and third and fourth and fifth competitors.

By doing that on a consistent basis, you can start to dominate the search engines for your most important keywords.

If you build out your site for your services and sub-services, optimize the pages using SEO best practices and then systematically obtain inbound links, you will start to DOMINATE the search engines for the plumbing related keywords in your area.

Content Marketing Strategies

Another highly important factor in SEO is relevant ongoing updates to your website. In the internet age, content is king.

Google loves fresh content. In some cases, with the changes in the algorithm, just because you've got a great website with the right title tags and all the best links, you may get discounted if they're not seeing fresh information posted on a consistent basis.

It is important to have a methodology where you are creating and posting content to your website on a regular basis. I want to give you a framework for figuring out what kind of content you could write, why you should create content, and how you can do it consistently.

First, you need to understand and accept that you need to become a subject matter expert. You might not consider yourself a writer or a content creator, but you are a subject matter expert.

There are things that you know that the general population does not. You're a plumber, a roofer, a pool builder and you have a team of people that are experts in this area, as well. You can create content on the topic that you know most about.

You can write about the differences between tank and tankless water heaters, why you would want to consider trenchless versus a regular project, or the differences between copper and PVC piping. There are a lot of different topics you can come up with that you can create content about.

Easy Content Creation

You should also consider that content doesn't have to be just written words. It's doesn't have to be just articles. Content can come in a variety of forms. The most popular are going to be articles, photos, videos and audio files. Stop and think about what content creation method works best for you.

Some people are great writers and that's their strength. Other people like to be on camera. I personally like to create videos. I'm very comfortable creating videos.

Other people can talk, and they can talk your ear off about whatever topic they are passionate about. You can create content in many different ways.

Because it is what I enjoy, I'll use video as an example. A contractor can set up a camera and record himself explaining the differences between using a tank and going tankless in the same manner that he would explain it to a customer.

Now you'll actually have multiple pieces of content. You'll have a video, which can be uploaded to YouTube, Vimeo, Metacafe, etc. That one piece of content can create multiple invaluable links to your website.

You can also take that video, save the audio portion of it, and you've got an audio clip. You can upload that audio file to your website and post on other various sites. You can use a transcription service like Castingwords.com, for instance, where you upload the audio or video file and somebody converts it to text.

For a couple of bucks, you'll have a complete article comprised of what you said. Now you've got a piece of content you can post to your blog. You can put it on eHow or one of those other article directory sites.

You want to create content on a consistent basis, using the blog on your website as the hub to post it, but then syndicating it to various sources. Syndicating it to article directory sites if it's in text form, and sending it to video sites like Vimeo, Metacafe and YouTube.com if it's in video form.

Doing this keeps the content fresh on your website/domain and creates a lot of authority, which is really going to help with the overall ranking of the website on the search engines.

You want to make sure you're appropriating each one of these link-building opportunities to maximize your rank-potential in your area. You might be surprised that contracting and home services are highly competitive from a SEO perspective.

There are a lot of contractors that want to rank for the same keywords, and many of them have invested heavily in the internet and in getting themselves higher in the search engines.

#6: Are You Optimized for Google Maps?

The next real big piece of the equation, and if we continue on our checklist, are you optimized for the Google Map listings?

This is critical. One of the most common questions I get from plumbing and HVAC companies every day is, "How do I get my company ranked on the Google Map in my market?"

There are really three core elements that go into getting ranked on the Google Map.

> ➢ **Claim your Google Listings**

> The first step is to make sure you have claimed and optimized Google My Business – www.google.com/business.

> ➢ **Citations or Web References**

> The second piece, which is actually more important than even having the listing optimized correctly, is the number of citations or web references of your company's name, address and phone number.

This is one of the things Google looks at.

If there are 110 plumbing companies in your city, and Google wants to determine who should be in spot A, versus spot B, versus spot D, there are algorithms looking for authority symbols or signals.

Those authority signals really point to whether that company is authentic; are they really at that location?

The way Google tells that is by looking across the web and seeing:

- o Are you on Angie's List?
- o Are you on Citysearch?
- o Are you on Best of the Web?
- o Are you on Hotfrog?
- o Are you on eLocal Plumber?
- o Are you on all of those little online directories with your company's name, address and phone number?

It's not even the paid listings, it's are you in those places?

There's about 250 online directories – a lot more than that, but 250 really authoritative online directories.

Are you in there?

Are you sure that you have consistency with your name, address and phone number?

To the extent that Google sees you're in those places with consistency of your name, address and phone number, that's an authority signal that Google looks at and says, "OK, this is a quality company that should be ranked well on the Google Map listings."

> **Online Reviews**

The other critical element of getting ranked in the Map listings is online reviews.

We find that, all other things being equal, the companies that have the most authentic, real reviews from their real customers, tend to rank best.

So it's imperative that you put a strategy in place to make sure you're in all of the online directories.

Do you have a proactive strategy in place for getting online reviews on a consistent basis?

You should have a strategy for consistently getting new reviews from your real customers in your true service area.

Getting Your Strategy in Place

I'm telling you with a very high degree of confidence, if you do those three things, and you don't try and overthink it, you don't overcomplicate it, you will move to a very prominent position on the Maps in your area.

> **If you do those things, and you don't overcomplicate it, you will move to a very prominent position on the Maps in your area.**

This is an extremely important part of creating a dominant presence on the internet so over the next few pages, I will provide more detail in a Special Briefing.

SPECIAL BRIEFING: GOOGLE MAPS OPTIMIZATION

In this Special Briefing, we'll break down the elements of being optimized for Google Maps and go into depth with you on how to do these different pieces.

Before we dive into this, I want to let you know about a Google Maps cheat sheet that we developed.

This cheat sheet basically takes that to-do list and gives you a specific plan of attack on how to make sure you've done everything that you should do to put your best foot forward on Google My Business.

If you want to download the cheat sheet, you can simply go to www.plumberseo.net/cheat-sheet, and you'll get to a place where you can download it.

PART ONE: YOUR GOOGLE LISTING

Step #1: Claim the Listing

The first thing you'd want to do is go to Google.com/business and either claim or update your Google My Business listing.

I'm going to assume, if you're reading this book, that you've got a Google Map listing and you're going to be working off some existing information that's on the Web.

If you're not, adding yourself to the Google Map is a very simple process.

You would just go to the same page (www.google.com/business) and click, "Add listing," and you would add your details, and Google will walk you step-by-step through that process. That's all done at Google.com/business.

Assuming you do, like I said, have an active listing, there's going to be one thing you need to know. That's your username and password that was used to claim your Google Map listing.

Whether you claimed that listing on Google Places or you actually did it on Google+ Local, you should have a Gmail account and password or an email account and password that would take you into your Google My Business listing.

If you don't, I'm going to encourage you that you find whoever it was that claimed the listing for you, whether it was an outsourced provider or an independent party.

I would reach out to them and say, "I need to get my Google username and password that you used to claim my Map listing so that I can get in and make the necessary updates, make sure I'm optimized correctly, and make sure that I have the right information on my Google My Business profile." I don't think there's any conflict of interests here.

> Google is the number one place people are looking when they need your services.

This is your company. Google is the number one place people are looking when they need your services.

There should be no reason that they wouldn't be able to provide you that username and password. You can just go in and double check your settings.

Step #2: Check the Information

A couple of things you want to do within the listing. When you get into Google.com/business, you will get to a page that looks like this.

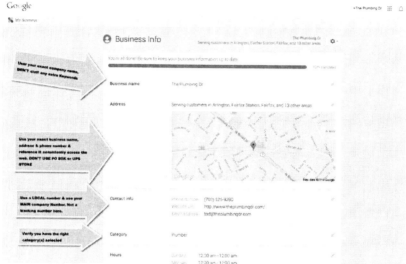

You can hit the edit button. You've got control of certain things.

You can change your name and your business address that's in your contact information.

Some very specific things I want you to pay attention to in Google My Business to make sure that you're following the rules and that you don't have anything that's going to prevent you from ranking well on the Google Map.

- Company Name

The first thing, which is pointed to at the very top, is your company name.

This seems pretty obvious, "Oh, my company name is what it is," but you'd be surprised.

If I looked at 20 different Google My Business listings, probably 11 or 12 of them have incorrect information on the company name.

That's because a year ago, two years ago, it was pretty popular to say, "Here's my company name. I'm going to put a little dash, and I'm also going to include additional keywords. Instead of the Plumbing Doctor, I'll put the Plumbing Doctor – Falls Church Plumber to try and get additional keywords in the company name field because, oh golly, that's going to tell Google that I should rank for more keywords."

That, in today's market, is a major no-no. You want to make sure you look at that business name field and make sure it's just your company name with no additional information.

- Company Address

Below that, you've got the address and the information about where you serve. Use a real business address here.

Don't try and use a P.O. Box, or a Mail Boxes Etc. or a UPS Store address. There was a time you could do that. You could have a different P.O. Box address in multiple different markets and start to rank in five, six, seven different cities.

Google really wants to serve real, authentic information. That's why they're looking at the consistency of the name, address, and phone number. That's why they're looking across the Web.

I'm pretty confident now they've got a database of the P.O. boxes, and the Mail Boxes Etc. and the UPS Stores. They're flagging those addresses that clearly aren't true locations and dropping them out of search.

I haven't seen it with my clients, but I have seen it with other people that do this on their own where they've basically fallen out of the Map listings because they were using a fake address. Use a real authentic address.

Ideally, it is your warehouse, the actual physical location that you work out of, or in the worst-case scenario, a virtual office where you have a unique address with a unique suite number that's not shared by any other companies, and that you can list, and Google would recognize. It needs to be a place also where you receive mail.

The big "gotcha" there is don't use a P.O. Box. Very rarely do we see P.O. Boxes rank well in the Map listings.

- Company Phone Number

You need to use a local number here in the phone number field. When you're looking at this section, you're looking at how your number is being referenced on the Web.

- Don't use an 800 number.
- Don't use a tracking number.

A lot of companies are moving towards tracking everything. "Let's have a tracking number on Google Maps. Let's have a tracking number on Yelp. Let's have a tracking number on Citysearch." It's very easy and cost effective to get a new number for each one of these directories.

What we're finding is Google considers your name, address, and phone number your thumbprint.

It should be the same across the Web. If that thumbprint matches up, and it's the same on Google, and Yahoo, and Bing, and Citysearch, and Angie's List, Google says, "OK. This is authentic, and this listing should rank well on the Map listings."

However, if you're using different tracking numbers throughout all of your different online directories and on your website, it will be a mismatch, since Google tries to find a consistent name, address, phone number match.

If it's a mismatch in every place they look, this could be a reason that your company might not wind up ranking as well as it could in the Map listings.

If you are going to use tracking, try and pick one online tracking number, "This is going to be the tracking number that I use."

Use that same number on Google, on your website, on Citysearch, on

Yelp.com, on Angie's List.

That way, at least Google can find that consistency. However, better than that is to use your real, authentic number, the one that you set up way back in the day when you first started your business. That's the best practice: using your real authentic phone number.

Step #3: Choosing Categories

In categories, if we're talking about a plumbing company, it would be plumber. If it was an HVAC company, it would be air conditioning contractor. It used to be Google had a number of different categories. With this latest change in Google My Business, they really narrowed it down.

You want to find the one category that applies to your business. Maybe two or three, if it's there.

Google is not letting you create your own categories now. You have got to choose the category; the bucket that makes sense.

As you're looking through this, just look at that category and make sure it's correct.

Step #4: Add Hours of Operation

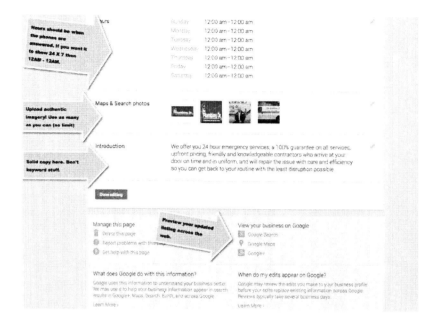

Below that, we have our hours of operation. If you're a true 24/7 provider, where you're answering the phones, and you can dispatch 24/7, you want to use 12:00 AM to 12:00 AM. That way, it's showing it.

If you only answer the phones between 8:00 AM and 6:00 PM or 7:00 PM, you probably want to put that in that area, because Google doesn't like the sense that somebody could think that you're open, and try and call, and not get a live answer.

You will find, though, if you put 8:00 AM to 6:00 PM, and you look at your Google Map listing or your Google My Business listing, at one of those times outside those hours it will say, "This business is closed."

If you're a true 24/7 service, you want to make sure your hours in the Google My Business listing reflects that.

Step #5: Add Pictures and Images

You now have the ability to upload as many pictures as you want. If you've been through Google Places or Google+ Local, on Google Places you were limited to 10 photos. You wanted to try and maximize those photos to the best of your ability.

With Google My Business, it's really unlimited. It's tied to Google+ now. You can add as many pictures as you want.

Another best practice is how you're going to use imagery on your Google My Business listing to be as authentic as possible. It's easy to upload 15 or 20 pictures that have no resonance, that don't really have any value. Try and have your logo, a picture of the owner, a picture of the team, a picture of the trucks, a picture of the office, a picture of your equipment.

> **Go for the opportunity to put your real people in the pictures.**

All these pictures or all these images are authentic. If somebody gets to the listing, they get to see a sense of what your company is really all about, as opposed to just stock photography.

When you have the choice between, "Do I put a picture of my truck stacked up, or do I put a picture of the team in front of our building, or, better, the team all standing in front of the truck in a group?" go for the latter. Go for the opportunity to put your real people in the pictures in that area.

One of the things I get push-back on in terms of images sometimes is, "Oh well, you know we've got 30 guys, but we've got a lot of turnover, so I don't want to take a picture of my team because then I'll have to change it again every single month."

That's a great way to never get anything done. "Oh, you know, I don't want to take the picture because eventually I'll have a totally different team. Don't worry about people leaving. The picture is a representation of the team. It does not need to be 100 percent up to date at any given moment to be an example of your team. People are not going to come to the office or call you guys out on a service call and say, "Hey, where's this guy, I didn't see him within your company?"

That's not the point. Just go ahead and get the team together, even if it's not the entire team, get in front of your trucks, take that picture that resonates a lot. Those are the types of images you want to put there in the picture area on the Google My Business listing.

Step #6: Write the Introduction

In terms of the introduction, you have a lot of room to put copy here. Don't use this as an opportunity to stuff, "Plumber", "Plumbing", "Emergency Plumber", "Drain Cleaning", "Water Heater Repair".

Use intelligent copy that speaks to somebody that's trying to choose a plumbing company, or a HVAC company, or whatever service you provide. Use that area to write a compelling message, "We offer 24 hour emergency service", "100 percent guarantee", "Up-front pricing", "Friendly, knowledgeable contractor who arrives at your door, on time, and in uniform."

Use that kind of language, instead of keyword stuffed language.

Step #7: View the Business

One of the cool things now with Google My Business is down towards the bottom – where you'll see the last arrow on the page – you have the opportunity to see what your business actually looks like in Google search, on Google Maps and on Google+.

After you update your listing, hit the "Done Editing" button. Check out how your listing is showing across the Web, and it gives you a good idea of what you're going to look like after Google runs its update, within a two to three day period.

Avoiding Duplicates

Beyond the basics of claiming your Map listing, one of the reasons we see companies not ranking in the Map listing is because there's duplicates.

Google says, "What's the company name, what's their address, what's their phone number?" Somehow along the way there was more than one listing created. Maybe it was intentional. Maybe it was by accident. When Google finds duplicates, sometimes it drops both listings out altogether.

What you want to do is you want to look, if you log into your Google My Business portal, sometimes you'll see something like this where there's two listings in the dashboard, and you want to get rid of the duplicate one. It's not adding any value, it's not showing up on anyone's search, and you want to erase it.

It wasn't all that self-explanatory to do this, so I created some snap-shots for you to follow along, when and if you see this in your dashboard.

- Hit the "Listing", up at the top you'll see a red banner that says, "This page has been blocked", because it's possibly spam or duplicate.
- You would hit the "Verify" button. Scroll down to the bottom, there's a "Delete This Page" option.
- After the dialogue box delete the page, check-box everything out, hit "Delete".

Obviously don't rush into this. If you're not 100 percent sure that that's the duplicate listing, and that's the one that needs to be updated, cool your jets, make sure that you've got the right one.

You don't want to accidentally delete your primary Map listing.

Information About Your Business

We talked about how to claim and optimize your Google My Business listing; you want to go in and follow that process.

Now the second one is establishing your name, address and phone number across the Web with consistency of how you're being referenced.

There is a wide range of different places and data providers which Google looks at to determine who you are as a company.

There's things like:

- Universal Business Listing
- Facebook
- Twitter
- Kudzu
- Citysquare
- eLocalPlumbers
- Angie's List
- Yelp

These are all online profiles, or online directories that list companies.

Google wants to see that you're in these various places, because if you're not, are you a brand new company? Are you not legit? However, if you are, then you must be a solid organization.

What I see in a lot of cases though, and the reason I say establish consistency of your name, address and phone number, is the following. I find companies that are very large, very well established, and who have been in their area for quite some time, but they don't rank well on the Google Map listings.

What has happened is there's a lot of fragmentation of how they're being referenced on the Web.

If we go into Kudzu, they're listed with one name, address and phone number, but if we look at Yelp, it's a different name, address and phone number. If we look at Hotfrog it's some variation thereof.

You need to spend some time, if you're really going to rank well on the Google Map listings, isolating what's my true company name, address and phone number? How do I want to be referenced online?

Then go into each of these online profiles, one by one, and make sure that you've got that consistent so Google's not seeing fragmentation. Instead, they're seeing this is all one company, and this is how they're referenced across the Web.

We found that when you get that right the way that you rank on the Google Map listings is significantly stronger.

Some of the citations that you want to make sure you pay attention to include:

- Bing Local
- Citysearch
- Yahoo
- Angie's List
- Judy's Book
- Local.com
- Merchantcircle
- YP.com
- DexKnows

There's a lot of online directories that apply to your plumbing or HVAC business.

There's actually probably about 250. You want to make sure that you're in the major online directories with the right information.

Best Practices

Again just to recap some of those best practices:

- Company name should just be your company name.
- Add your Website address, it's a great link.
- Don't use 800 numbers.
- Use your real, physical location as opposed to a PO Box, or a Mail Boxes Etc. or a UPS store.
- Upload pictures. Leverage personality.
- Pay attention to your categories and your hours of operation. Make sure it matches up with the reality of your company.

PART TWO: IMPROVING YOUR RANKING

So what are the new ranking factors that determine where you appear?

Well, Google does not publish a document that says, "This is how we determine what's going to rank in the Google Map listings." They don't publish any of that.

So this is conjecture based on all the blog posts that are out there, all of the recent information on what Google is looking at to determine what's going to rank well on Maps.

It's also based on our experience with our clients, testing what works and what doesn't.

This is what we think are going to be some of the new ranking factors, outside of what was prior to the Google My Business being updated.

Number of Followers

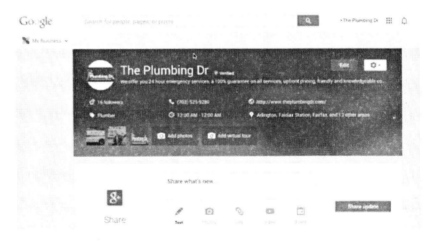

The first is the number of Followers. I'm going to show you in a visual, how you can see how many people are following your local business.

We think that that number is going to be a factor in rankings.

That's not to say you should go on fiverr.com and purchase 10,000 Followers, because Google does look at the Follower profile.

If you've got a business that's in Falls Church, Virginia and you've got 6,000 Followers and 90 percent of them are outside of Falls Church, or they're outside of even the United States, Google knows. Google has the IP address of the person's profile. They also have, is that a real person? Do they actually use Google profile? Do they have Gmail? Are they on YouTube? What's the IP address that they're checking in from on a consistent basis?

Quality is more important than quantity here. You want to put a strategy in place to get your real, authentic customers that have Google accounts to follow you and not just a bunch of bogus accounts.

Frequency of Posts

We think that Google's going to be looking at the frequency of posts. Google My Business is directly connected to Google+, which is the social media platform for your business on Google.

We think that having consistent updates being pushed out is going to be a factor, as well as the engagement of the Followers.

If you're putting out a daily post, and a couple times a day somebody replies, "Oh, wow that's really cool," or "Thanks for sharing that," we think that's going to be a factor in how Google determines whether you're an authentic business, in the true service area that you claim.

If you're authentic and you're more authoritative, that means you're going to potentially rank better in the Map listings.

Reviews

Then the other one – which I have listed here as a new ranking factor, but it's not all that new – reviews have always been a big piece of the equation in ranking.

But number of online reviews – and same with Followers – not just the quantity of reviews.

Real reviews from people with real online profiles, in your true service area, I think that all these variables are going to be very important; things you want to pay very close attention to as far as how you're going to be marketing yourself through Google My Business.

> **Real reviews from people with real online profiles, in your true service area are going to be very important.**

We'll look at reviews more closely in the next segment.

Tracking Your Data

There's a visual here of "The Plumbing Doctor" of Falls Church, Virginia, and in the top left you can see the number of Followers.

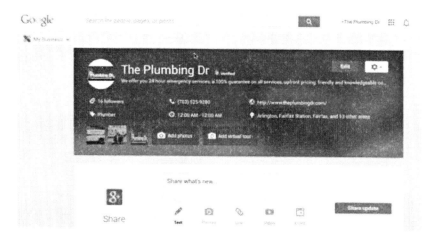

I think that's going to be an important factor: you want to make sure that you're getting that number as high as possible, with your real customers in your true service area.

Right within the Google My Business dashboard you're able to see your online reviews. You're not only able to see what your star rating is, and how many reviews you have on Google, Google is also now scouring the Web and pulling in your reviews from other sites, like YP.com and merchantcircle.com.

That 71 reviews from across the Web really is a pretty cool indication of how many reviews you have that Google's recognizing. That's a major factor in how your company is going to rank in the Google Map listings.

One cool feature here is when you click that "Manage Reviews" button. You'll see your reviews on Google. You can respond to them right there within the dashboard, which is great.

If someone says something positive, spend a few minutes to leave a response such as, "Hey, thanks for the review, really appreciate the opportunity to serve you."

If they write something negative you should still respond. You can write back with something like, "Hey, I'm really sorry to hear things didn't work out, we're trying to provide the best service possible. What could we have done differently?"

Being proactive with how you respond to even negative feedback can have a great impact on how people perceive you in your marketplace.

Right there within "Insights" you can see how many people saw your listing, how many people clicked on it, how many new Followers you have.

This is cool to look at, but really what I want to emphasize in this section is that Google is tracking this stuff.

Google has the data, they can see how many clicks you got on your listing, they can see how many Followers and what the velocity of new Followers is. If Google can track it, they can definitely apply it to their algorithm.

> **If Google can track it, they can definitely apply it to their algorithm.**

You want to pay close attention to see if you are getting new Followers to that Google My Business listing on a consistent basis. Are people interacting with what you're posting?

Some of things we know, the tried and true ranking factors, these things go back years and years. What we've found really determine whether a company will rank on page one, or whether they're going to be ranking on page six or page seven.

It's really about having a claimed and optimized Google listing on Google My Business, having lots of citations that reference your company's name, address and phone number, and having online reviews.

Ranking Problems

If you're not ranking on the Google Map right now if someone types in your city, it's probably because you're listing is not authoritative enough.

It goes back to the same three steps we discussed.

- Do you have it properly clean on the Google Map listings? Had you cleaned up any duplicate listings that might exist would Google drop you out?
- Do you have citations? Is Google just seeing you on Google My Business or are they seeing you all across the web?
- Do you have several legitimate, positive online reviews?

If you've got 20 or 30 or 60 or 70 other companies right in your same neighborhood that provide the same services, Google has to determine who's going to be in spot A versus spot D versus spot G.

All of those things being equal, the company that has more citations, has more followers, has more positive online reviews appears to be more authoritative. That's what Google is going to serve because they want their customer who's searching on Google, looking for information, to get the best information possible.

> **Google wants their customer who's searching to get the best information possible.**

Our cheat sheet gives you step-by-step what you need to do with the recent changes in the Google My Business. You can download the sheet at plumberseo.net/cheat-sheet.

That should really help drive what you need to be doing as far as claiming it, making sure that you don't have any infractions, making sure that you cleaned up your duplicates and putting a process in place to get your online reviews.

I can say with a high degree of confidence, if you follow this process and you do these things, you'll be well on your way to ranking very well in the Map listings in your market.

PART THREE – ONLINE REVIEWS

We talked about claiming the Map listing and we talked about establishing consistency of your name, address, and phone number, being in the online directories.

We also mentioned that the next really critical element is online reviews. So how do you get real reviews from your real customers in your true service area?

The best way to do it is to have a process in place where you're asking for reviews on a consistent basis. There's a lot of tools that can help automate this. I'm going to be talking about a tool that I think works really well. Even if you don't have any technology, if you're not doing anything fancy, all you have to do is develop the process and systematize it in your business.

What we find to be a good practice is to do it in two different ways.

Contacting All Past Customers

The first way, or the first pass, is to develop the names and email addresses of all of your customers, your sphere of influence, your past customers and put it into a simple document like an Excel spreadsheet.

Put together a basic email that just says, "Hey, thank you so much for your business throughout the years. We appreciate the opportunity to serve you. We're in the process of trying to develop our reputation online and we'd love if you'd take a few minutes to write us a review."

Give them the direct link to the various places where they can write your review.

Of course, not everyone has a Google account, and not everyone wants to create a Google account just to write a review for you. I don't necessarily think you want to force them to Google. You want to give them options. In that email you would say:

- Click here to get to our Google listing.
- Click here to get to our Angie's List listing.
- Click here to get to our YP.com listing.
- Click here to get to our Yelp listing.

Give them five or six options, and people will gravitate to the online profile that's most comfortable for them.

If they're a Yelp user and they write Yelp reviews after every restaurant that they go to, they're going to see that Yelp link and just jump right on Yelp.

Give them options and let them choose. That's the first pass. Send an email out to the customer base stating, "Thanks for your business. We'd love it if you'd write us a review."

Here is a template you can use for emailing your existing customers to request online reviews:

Email Subject: Thanks for your business!

Name,

I wanted to shoot you a quick email to thank you for your business and let you know how much we appreciate the opportunity to serve you!

Our goal is to provide 100% customer satisfaction and exceed your expectations every step of the way. I certainly hope that we did just that! If so, it would really help us out if you'd be willing to post a review for us online at one of your favorite online review sites. Below are a few direct links where you could write a public review about your experience with us:

- Google –
  https://plus.google.com/105923821769482824984
- Yelp –
  http://www.yelp.com/biz/carolina-deck-and-fence-charlotte
- Angie's List –
  http://www.angieslist.com/companylist/us/nc/charlotte/carolina-deck-and-fence-inc-reviews-336039.htm

Thank you again! We really appreciate your support!

Best Regards,
Luke Chapman
Lukes Plumbing, Heating & Air

Systematic Review Processes

The second pass, and I think probably the more important effort, is to make sure you've got a process where you're systematically thanking your customers after service and giving them options on how to write you a review.

In that specific vein, we're trying to take two approaches.

The first is the analog approach. Print out some business cards or some post cards or thank you cards and say, "Thanks for your business. We'd love it if you'd write us a review. If you would, go to yourcompany.com/reviews." On that page have those links where they can write you a review.

That's an easy process. Now, your technicians are trained after the service to say, "Thank you so much for your business. Here's a card. If you'd take a few minutes to write us a review, we would really appreciate it. All you have to do is go to this website address and choose the profile that you like and write us a review. We would really appreciate that."

That in and of itself will increase the number of reviews that you're getting on a consistent basis even if that's all you did.

Now, the way to take that to a level that is going to generate even more reviews is to send an email after service.

Have a template developed. Setup either MailChimp or Constant Contact or just a basic web form on your website where you can enter the customer's name and email address and, after every service call, have that email go out.

"Thank you so much for your business. We appreciate the opportunity to serve you. Our goal is to provide 100 percent customer satisfaction and if we didn't deliver that, please give me a call and let us know. If you had a great experience, we'd love it if you'd share that and, if you would, go to one of these various places to write us a review."

That's not super hard, something you can setup.

Just have an email go out after each service call and you'd be amazed at how the velocity of reviews that you have within your business increases.

Ideally, we want to get your technicians involved in this process. They're checking in, then they go back to their smartphone, they hit the "Request Review" button, and an email that's already queued up goes out to the customer.

We've found this to be a very effective way to make requesting and getting reviews a systematic part of your business.

If you think how many service calls you're doing on a daily basis, and you think, "If we had an email going out after every service call, would the number of reviews that we get online increase?"

It's unquestionable. The answer to that question is yes. That really helps with your rankings.

Your Systematic Process

You need to have a systematic process in place where you are asking for reviews on a consistent basis from the customers that you are serving on a daily basis. The best way to do that is to request an email address from your customers, either at point of service or after service.

We have found that the best time to ask for that email address is at the point of booking the service. If you wait until after the service is rendered your technicians on-site will say "OK, thanks for the money, by the way give me your email address".

They are going to say, "Why do you need my email address?" "Oh, because I want to ask you for a review or..." There is a lot of resistance to it at that point in the sales funnel.

However, if you move it to the front where somebody calls in and says, "Hey I need to schedule a service, my house is flooded," you can respond, "We can get somebody out there right away. Let me gather your information." This is the perfect time to get the email address.

Typically, you get their name, address, and the phone number. Just add one more step at that point and request an email address as well. You can tell them that it is so you can send a confirmation.

That's how you start to develop a database of emails. You need an email address so that you can send a message after service thanking them for their business and asking them to write you a review.

The number of reviews that you have from actual customers is going to increase exponentially if you repeat this process regularly.

This is how you are going to start to really dominate the Google Map, because reviews and citations work in harmony for ranking.

Here is a Sample Review Request Card

Have your technicians hand these out after each service call.

**We Hope You Are Satisfied
With The Service We
Provided Today.**

All Purpose Plumbing

Positive reviews help us out, we would appreciate it if you would be so kind as to leave us a review on Google + Local. Please go to this URL and leave us a review.

http://www.allpurposeplumbing.com/reviews/

Sample Review Request eMail

Put a system in place to send email like this after each service call.

Name,

I wanted to shoot you a quick email to thank you for your business and let you know how much we appreciate the opportunity to serve you!

Our goal is to provide 100% customer satisfaction and exceed your expectations every step of the way. I certainly hope that we did just that! If so, it would really help us out if you'd be willing to post a review for us online at one of your favorite online review sites.

Below are a few direct links where you could write a public review about your experience with us:

- Google – https://plus.google.com/105923821769482824984
- Yelp – http://www.yelp.com/biz/carolina-deck-and-fence-charlotte
- Angie's List – http://www.angieslist.com/companylist/us/nc/charlotte/carolina-deck-and-fence-inc-reviews-336039.htm

Thank you again! We really appreciate your support!

Best Regards,
Luke Chapman
Luke's Plumbing Heating & Air

Sample 'Review Us' landing page for your website

You want to direct your customers to a page like the one that follows, making it easy for them to write reviews on your various online review listings.

When I'm talking about optimizing for the Google Map listing, Google is not just showing your Google Map listings reviews, they're showing reviews that happened on YP.com, on Citysearch.com, on Yelp.com.

Google has the ability to pull the reviews from across the web, and they're looking at the overall online reputation, not just your Google My Business reputation. Let people choose the review profile where they want to write those reviews and get them online.

Leveraging Technology

One of the tools that we found that would be real beneficial for getting online reviews is to leverage technology.

There is a system we're using right now called Nearby Now. We tend to implement this for our clients. It runs on mobile devices.

It is set up so that Google understands what your true service area is.

As a plumbing or HVAC business, you're not like a dentist; you're not like an auto repair shop where you have a physical location and your customers come to you. Google, in that case says, "This is your address. You're probably within a 5 to 10 minute radius."

If you're a service provider that goes out to people's homes, it's a totally different thing. Google doesn't really know:

- Do you serve a 5-mile radius?
- Do you serve a 50-mile radius?
- Do you serve a 30 mile radius?

You want to do something to help Google understand what your true service area is.

The concept of Nearby Now is your technicians, for the most part, have smartphones. They have Android phones, they have iPhones. Ideally, you would have them install this application on their phone and as they're going about their day, they would take out the phone and they would check in.

The check-in data with location from where that check-in took place would be captured because all these phones now have GPS coordinates. Through a piece of code, you can now pull that check-in information onto your website and have a hit map that shows your service area, based on where true authentic check-ins are taking place, on a heat map.

Google looks at schema. It looks at hCard format. I'm not going to get too technical on this, but when Google spiders your website and then gets to your home page or it gets to one of your city pages, it can see where your team is checked-in with hCard and schema data behind it based on real, authentic check-ins. We found that to be a real powerful way for Google to understand what your true service area is.

Local Content

Through the technology, that information they checked in with will automatically syndicate to your website and to the sub-city pages on your website.

We talked about having pages for each one of the sub-cities that you operate in, and the fact that those sub-city pages need to have unique information and unique content.

This gives you a great way to create authentic, hyper local content, without having to completely reinvent the wheel on every page of your website.

That's the first phase of this. Your technicians are out in the field, they're doing something like 5, 10, 15, 20 service calls a day. As they're providing that service, they're checking in.

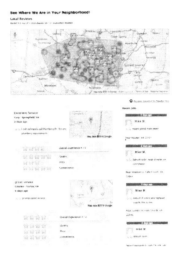

That's creating good, relevant content for your website.

They're typing a brief description.

Maybe it was a re-pipe, or they were quoting a water heater change out, or they were unclogging a drain.

Whatever it was, they type that brief description and now you've got good unique content for that page on your website as illustrated here, with hCard format information behind it.

It's passing really strong signals to Google, "This is my real service area. I'm not lying. My technicians have gone to this area, they've provided this service."

This really gives Google a strong indication of the area that you serve.

Reputation Monitoring

The other cool thing we like to implement on the back end of this is a reputation monitoring system or reputation filtering system.

The way it works is, first of all, the system will scour the web, like what Google is doing now with Google My Business, and find all your reviews.

It will find the ones in Angie's List and Citysearch and Yelp, for example, and it also provides a widget that you can put on your reviews page that shows all those reviews, where they're happening across the web.

It will say, "Right now, you have 70 reviews." Then it goes from 70 to 71 to 72 to 75, continuing to update as new reviews are added. The reviews page on the site also gets updated with that new testimonial.

Now, you're showing your customers, when they get to the site, this is a really authoritative company. Look, how good we are. Look at the great service we provide.

The cool thing about it is as customers write new reviews, and if you've got a process in place where you're giving a manual card, "Please write us a review," and you're sending an email after every service call, you're going to get more reviews.

Now, you really want to be paying attention to what people are saying. Are they saying good things? Are they saying bad things? What's happening? It will let you know.

You get an email that says you just got a review on Yelp or you just got a review on Angie's List – good, bad or indifferent.

If it's four stars or higher, if it's a good review, it will showcase that on your website. They will hit that little sidebar that the red arrows point to and will update on the reviews page of your website.

It's really powerful stuff to help showcase the positive information that's happening within your company.

It also serves as a reputation filter of sorts. If you do get that errant one-star review or two-star review, you'll get an email, you'll be alerted that there's a bad review, and you can take action.

If you do get that one-star or that two-star review, you can address it immediately and either talk to the customer offline or in a public space, write, "Hey, we're really sorry. What can we do to make this right?"

A negative review can really have a very positive impact if you handle it correctly.

It's just as important to take action on the negative reviews as it is on the positive reviews.

Proven Results

In the case of The Plumbing Doctor case study I mentioned earlier, they weren't ranking well on the Google Map.

- We had done everything.
- We had claimed their Map listing.
- We had developed their citations.
- We had made sure there was consistency of their name, address and phone number.

But it was still eluding them.

They were still just ranking in the organic listings.

We got this process in place, and because they did so many service calls and they started to leverage the technology, the number of reviews that they had on Google Maps and across the web – 39 reviews on the Google Map listings and 170+ across the web – they jumped to a very strong placement in the Google Map listings.

#7: Are You Active on Social Media?

The next question is, are you active in social media? When I say social media, I'm talking about:

- Facebook
- Twitter
- Google Plus
- LinkedIn
- YouTube

When I talk to other plumbing and HVAC business owners, I often get a blank stare. They say: "I know that there's lots of kids on Facebook, and I know there's lots of people using Twitter, but I don't understand how that's going to apply to my business. I don't see how that's going to help me in any way."

The way I like to explain it, and the way I like to help emphasize the value of social media, is by asking, "Right now, if you just stop and

> Social media is a tremendous avenue for taking repeat and referral business to the next level.

think, what's the number one source of business for your company?"

If you've been around for any period of time, if you have a strong company, I can say 90 percent of the time that the answer to that is repeat and referral business.

It's your previous customers using you again, and it's your previous customers referring you to their friends and others.

More Repeat Business & More Referrals

Social media is a tremendous avenue for taking that repeat and referral business to the next level, and really maximizing that word of mouth and repeat and referral business.

The reason I say that is because there are 1.6 billion users on Facebook; the average user has 135 friends and checks in between six and nine times per day.

- 1.6 Billion Users
- Average user has 135 Fiends
- Check's in 6-9 X per day

If you can get a strategy or a process in place to get your real customer – not some random person in a faraway country or some random individual out in cyberspace, but your real customer base, the people that would refer you, the people that have used you in the past – to press "Like," by virtue of that "like," they've exposed you to 135 of their friends.

It's almost as if they've handwritten a note that said, "Hey, I found this great plumbing or HVAC company in our market. The next time you need those types of services, I really highly recommend these guys."

In addition to that, they've given you permission to remain top of mind with them.

They're checking in between six and nine times per day. As long as you're putting out relevant, non-obtrusive, non-obnoxious updates on a consistent basis, every time they check into Facebook to see what's going on with the grandkids or to connect with friends, they see your logo.

That remains top of mind. They're seeing you more often.

Do you think if they're seeing you a couple times a week as a result of the posts you're putting out on Facebook, they're more likely to remember you the next time they need a plumber? Or the next time somebody asks if they know a good HVAC repair company?

That's really, in my mind, the power of social media.

You want to make sure you're set up on Facebook, Twitter, Google Plus, LinkedIn, and that you're updating those profiles often.

Daily would be ideal, weekly would be a minimum.

What's the point in having a lot of your real customers on social media, if you're not putting out updates on a consistent basis?

The questions here are:

- Do you have business profiles for Facebook, Twitter, Google Plus and LinkedIn?
- How many "likes" do you have on Facebook?
- Are you updating your social media profiles on a consistent basis?

Another question that should be in there is, "Do you have a strategy to get your real customers to press "Like," to press "Subscribe," to press "Follow?"

#8: Are You Leveraging Email Marketing?

The next piece is, are you leveraging email marketing? When I'm talking about email marketing, I'm not asking if you have Outlook or if you send emails with quotes.

I'm really talking, do you have a strategy in place where you're collecting the names and email addresses of your customers, and are you sending out updates on a consistent basis to your sphere or to your past customers?

I like to explain this one with a story. I recently did an interview with Daniel Cordova Plumbing, out of the San Fernando Valley area in California. In my mind he's one of the fastest-growing plumbing companies in the United States.

He grew from zero to over $1 million within his first two years in business. Outstanding growth.

I asked him, "What's been the secret sauce? What's the main thing you can point to as a result of your success?" He said, "It's been twofold. The first is Internet, and getting my Internet strategy right. The second is leveraging effective email marketing."

What he did was, he has his dispatchers make sure that they collect the name and email address of every person that calls in. Whether they book a call or not, he's getting the name and he's getting the email address as often as he can.

Then, he sends out a monthly, personality-based newsletter, via email to that customer list.

Because he's remaining top of mind, because he's communicating in that way, he's improved his customer loyalty.

He's improved his referrals, and he's improved his repeat business. It's been a tremendous impact on his company.

Now, sending emails is one of the lowest cost ways to remain in contact with your customer base.

If you are not doing email marketing, you are missing a tremendous opportunity. What are some of the tools you can use for email marketing? Well, the most common ones are:

- Constant Contact
- Aweber
- Mail Chimp

These are low cost tools between $10 and $20 per month, that give you the ability to house the names and email addresses of your customers, put together nice email newsletters, and push them out on a monthly basis.

I highly encourage you to leverage email marketing to send a newsletter, but then there's other things you can do with email.

The first is to send an email after every service call to request reviews.

We talked about the importance of having online reviews from your real customers in your true service area.

What better way to get those reviews than to make sure an email goes out after every service call requesting a review and making it easy?

The second, why not leverage email as a tool to get your customers to engage with you on social media?

There is no reason you can't send an email a week after service, or two weeks after service. Just say, "Hey, we're really active on social media. We've got a great following and we'd love to have you join our online community."

That's a great way to get that engagement and get those real customers to press the "Like" button.

Of course, sending a monthly newsletter – something informational, maybe a special offer along with it – is a great way to leverage email within your online marketing strategy.

So are you leveraging email marketing?

- Do you have a database where you're collecting email addresses?
- Are you sending out an email newsletter?
- Are you leveraging email to get online reviews and to draw customers into your social media profiles?

If you're not, this is a very low cost way to remain in contact and to really take your business to the next level.

Building Strong Foundations Before Buying Advertising

Everything we've talked about to this point is all foundational. It's things like:

- Setting up your website
- Optimizing it for the search engines
- Making sure that it's compelling
- Making sure it's got the right conversion elements
- Having a strategy to get online reviews
- Being properly optimized for the Google Map listing
- Leveraging email marketing and social media

None of these tools are really advertising. They're just part of an effective online marketing strategy.

You have to have them in place, and you need to be doing them right. I always like to emphasize that they should be the foundation of your online marketing strategy.

The pyramid that I have, below, goes from the bottom to the top: being organic, being social, having paid directories, and pay-per-click.

What I'm really trying to communicate here is:

You should never even consider paid online advertising, pay-per-click advertising, or paid ads, before you have the foundation right.

The reason for that is, if you don't have your website set up correctly, if you don't have online reviews, if you don't have compelling messaging that makes somebody choose you versus the competition, then why would you want to pay to get people to your website?

You're going to be wasting dollars that aren't going to convert correctly.

The other reason is that I've found the quality of the traffic you get from being properly optimized and

> I've found that the quality of the traffic you get from being properly optimized and ranking in the non-paid listings is significantly greater.

ranking in the non-paid listings is significantly greater.

Usually, once you get that piece of the equation right, you're going to have additional leads. You're going to have additional revenues. You're going to have additional profits that you can and will want to reinvest into the business, but not until you have the foundation right.

So many times I've talked to plumbing and HVAC contractors, and they have this pyramid inverted.

- They're spending a lot of money in pay-per-click.
- They're heavily invested in YP.com and Angie's List.

BUT

- They don't have the website right.
- They don't have a proactive email or social media strategy.

I feel that it's a miss, so I want to make sure that you've thought about having a sound foundation and really building your online marketing strategy based on these principles.

#9: Are You Taking Advantage of Paid Online Marketing Opportunities?

Once you have those firm foundations in place and once you have them right, that's when it starts to make sense to look at paid online marketing initiatives like:

- Pay-per-Click campaigns
- Paid ads on Angie's List, YP or Yelp.com

The reason I mentioned those three online directories is because I've found them to be pretty effective.

With the clients that we work with, with the people that I interview as part of our plumbing marketing podcast (at PlumbingMarketing.net), very often Angie's List is referenced as a great source of the right kind of costumers. It's not cheap. Sometimes the people are obnoxious, but they're usually the right kind of customer that's not just out looking for the lowest price.

They're looking for quality, and they're willing to pay a premium to deal with a quality organization.

Successful Pay-per-Click

The fact is most pay-per-click campaigns fail.

As I talk to plumbing and HVAC contractors throughout the United States, a lot of them just say they gave up on pay-per-click.

They spent thousands of dollars. They got very little or no return on investment and it was a big failure for them.

I want to encourage you, that if you set up pay-per-click advertising correctly, it can be very effective and it can be profitable.

> *The reason most pay-per-click campaigns fail is because there is a failure to understand the way the AdWords auction process works.*

A lot of people think it's just a function of bids – that, if you pick your keywords and if you bid more than the other guy, you're going to be at the top. And that, if you are at the top, you're going to get the best results.

That doesn't take into account the fact that Google has a quality score in place. That quality score is really built to make sure that even the paid listings are relevant to the customer.

When the customer is looking for a plumber, a drain cleaning, a water heater installation, Google wants to serve relevant quality results – not just generic, boring or irrelevant information.

Most pay-per-click campaigns are set up with one ad group that covers all the plumbing keywords – plumbing, drain cleaning, water

> The quality score is built to make sure that even the paid listings are relevant to the customer.

heater installation, water heater repair, re-piping.

They bid on those keywords and all of those text ads land directly on the home page.

This is a recipe for failure because it's not relevant, either for Google or the end user.

If the customer is searching on hydro-jetting, it's not compelling when the customer gets to your home page that doesn't:

- Say anything about hydro-jetting
- Offer them a specific reason why they should choose you for their hydro-jetting job
- Offer a special promotion or incentive to use you for their hydro-jetting job

What happens is you spend a lot of money paying more for the click than you need to pay. Also, your conversion rate on those clicks is relatively low because it's not compelling and it doesn't speak to the specific question that the person asked when they ran their search.

So what's the right way to do this?

The right way to make sure you get the most out of your pay-per-click advertising budget is to be strategic and to set up specific ad groups for each one of your services.

- You group the plumbing-related keywords together, you group the emergency plumbing keywords together, and you group the drain cleaning keywords together.
- You write a specific text ad for those actual keywords.
- You land them on a specific page on your website that talks to that specific group of keywords.

By doing that, your quality score is better because you are more relevant.

Your cost per click is lower while still maintaining

top positioning and your conversion rate is higher because the customer got what they wanted.

Paid Online Marketing

If you are going to play the pay-per-click game – and I highly recommend that you do – do it when your foundation is strong. You have to make sure you do it in this way, that you are strategic with how you set it up. That's how it makes sense.

- Do you have AdWords set up?
- Are you specifically targeting with ad groups, text ads and landing pages?
- Do you have a premium ad on Angie's List, YP, and Yelp.com?
- Are you taking advantage potentially of pay-per-lead services like Home Adviser?

Now, notice how I mentioned that last. That is a throw away option if you just want to get some additional leads.

It's the lowest quality lead you can get. However, if you do it correctly and if you have a strategy specifically for those pay-per-lead options, it can be profitable.

By that I mean, you have somebody dedicated to respond to those leads the moment they come in and you're aggressive with the way that you follow up.

Maybe you have a lead follow up sequence in place for those people that you callback that you don't get live. Or they get a three-part email remaining top of mind until they do take action.

If you do it like this you can do a little bit better with those pay-per-lead services. However, it's definitely not where to start building your online marketing strategy.

Just revisiting our case study on The Plumbing Doctor, we talked about how they three-timed their leads and their sales by getting the fundamentals right.

That was all based on SEO, getting ranked in the organic listing and making sure the website was more compelling.

Then, as we started to implement some of these paid online strategies, the traffic to the website took another jump from 712 visitors to 1,092 visitors.

That resulted in an increase from 72 calls to 213 calls.

If we do a quick recap, when they started with us in 2011 they had 24 calls; by January 2014, they had 213 calls.

I talked about how I was going to show you how you can triple your sales. Well, that's an example of a company which, by implementing all of the strategies we talked about here, was able to 10x their sales.

If you really work through all these steps and all of these different strategies, you can feel confident that you can get similar, or possibly even greater results, in your plumbing and HVAC business.

In the Special Briefing that follows, I go into a lot more detail on how to set up and manage your PPC activity so it gives you the best possible return on your investment.

SPECIAL BRIEFING: PAY-PER-CLICK MARKETING

In this Special Briefing, we're going to look at why you should have pay-per-click marketing as part of your overall internet marketing strategy.

Benefits of Pay-Per-Click Marketing

Why should pay-per-click be part of your overall Internet marketing strategy? You can start to show up quickly. This is one the benefits of Google AdWords versus search engine optimization. You can say, "I'd like to make sure I'm showing up in my market when someone types in 'plumber,' 'plumbing,' 'AC repair,' 'air conditioning contractor.'"

With an AdWords campaign, you literally pick those keywords, you set up your text ads and you set up your landing pages. Within 24 hours, you can begin to start showing up in the paid listings for your keywords.

It also gives you the opportunity to show up as often as possible where people are looking for you. I mentioned earlier the differences between the paid listings, the Map listings, and the organic listings. We've got clients that if you search their city + plumber, they're the number one organic listing and they're also even showing up on the Google Map.

Either way, you want to show up as often on the page as possible for the keywords people are typing in when they need your services. Having a pay-per-click strategy in place gives you the ability to show up in the paid listings and then show up in the organic listings, as well. It gives you another placeholder.

Geographic Keywords

Another benefit of PPC is that it also gives you the opportunity to show up for non-geo-modified keywords. Google has been messing with the algorithm and showing more specific searches depending upon where you search from. However, for the most part, if we go to your computer right now, and we type in "plumber," "emergency plumber," "drain cleaning service," it's going to show the national results for those key terms.

You're going to be competing against national websites as opposed to just the people in your local area, versus if they typed in your city like: "Miami plumber," "Miami plumbing," "Miami emergency plumber." Of course, then you're competing against those other companies in your market that aren't going after the national work, they're going after the local work.

In a lot of cases, you won't show up for the non-geo-modified keywords. With the pay-per-click marketing strategy, you can. Let's use the example of someone who types in the keyword "emergency plumber." As long as they searched from, let's say a 20-mile radius of your office – and Google can do that based on the IP address of where they ran the search – you can be bidding and showing up in that section.

Importance of Mobile

Having a pay-per-click marketing element of your online marketing strategy does give you the opportunity to show up for more keywords. More and more people, as you know, are going to the Internet from their mobile devices, from their iPhones, their Android phones, and all the other mobile devices out there.

On mobile, if you run a search right now for your city plumber, you'll notice that a lot of the real estate is taken up by pay-per-click listings and only a little bit shows up in the organic.

> A pay-per-click marketing strategy helps you to show up for more keywords in mobile search.

I think the propensity for someone to click a paid listing is higher in a mobile search than it is in the desktop search.

With a pay-per-click strategy specifically targeting mobile, you can actually have it where it does click to call.

They see your text ad, they press the "Call" button, and it's calling your office right away. I believe having a pay-per-click strategy specifically set up for mobile devices is an essential piece of the puzzle and it's a great way to get calls.

These are some of the reasons you want to make sure that you have pay-per-click as part of your overall strategy, assuming you've got the foundation part of that really nice and tight.

The Different Pay-Per-Click Networks

There are a number of pay-per-click networks. The two main ones are Google AdWords and Microsoft Ads.

Those two ad networks will give you access to show up in the paid listings for almost all the search engines on the market; not all, but the ones that count.

Within Google AdWords and their search network, obviously you've got Google.com, but then you have AOL and Ask.com and CNN and USA Today. People search on some of those other sites, as well.

When you run a pay-per-click campaign on AdWords and their search network, that gives you a large audience where you can be showing up in the paid listings when someone types in "your city AC repair," "your city air conditioning contractor."

Within the Microsoft search network, you get Bing and Yahoo. Those two are both under that same umbrella along with some of the smaller tier-two type sites, also.

Where to Start

If you're thinking, "Where should I start? If I'm going to do pay-per-click advertising, where should I begin?" this chart shows that more than 80 percent of the search happens on Google and Google search network.

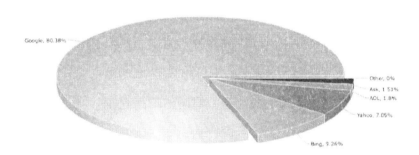

Search Engines Market Share

Google, 80.38%
Other, 0%
Ask, 1.51%
AOL, 1.8%
Yahoo, 7.05%
Bing, 9.26%

If you are going to start anywhere, start with Google, but there's still that other 20 percent of the market that's searching on Bing and on Yahoo.

Bing is getting a little bit of momentum. I wouldn't say it's huge momentum, but they're starting to get some momentum.

There's another slither of the pie that you probably want to look at.

The cost per click on Bing and Yahoo is quite a bit less. If you look at it overall, you can actually get a much lower cost per lead or cost per inbound phone call to your business on Bing and Yahoo, but there's only so much opportunity because it's only about 20 percent of the search volume.

That gives you an idea what the landscape is. Definitely, start with Google AdWords, but don't ignore Bing and Yahoo. If you've got a large budget and you're trying to really saturate your market, then definitely, you should be playing on both Bing and Google.

How the Process Works

Let's talk about how the AdWords auction process works. There's a lot of misinformation or misunderstanding about how this works. A lot of people think that the AdWords auction process is solely based on the cost per click.

They think, "Well, if I have the highest bid, then I'll be the number one guy, right? And that's all that really matters."

But the reality is Google has to serve relevant results. If they're going to serve relevant results, they can't just let the highest bidder get the top position. They have to have what they call a quality score. The above illustration shows the dollars way off.

Within plumbing, a top position is going to cost you more, in most markets, than $17 or $18 per click. In major markets, like Los Angeles, I've seen it significantly higher than that. However, what I want you to see is the number one person bid $2 and has the top spot versus the person below that could have bid $2.20 and have the second spot. It's because Google has to serve relevant results.

The best example of this that I've seen is if somebody were to go to Google and run a search for "BMW",

> **Google has to make sure that they're serving relevant results.**

obviously, they're looking for a BMW. That's what they're in the market for. However, if you think about this person's demographics, that this is a person who is looking for a luxury vehicle, probably a high-end shopper, and a pretty desirable shopper or searcher that a lot people would want to target their messaging to.

For all intents and purposes, Mercedes might say, "Well, if they're searching for "BMW", I'd like to bid $70 per click and be the number one result for "BMW." That doesn't create a good experience for the searcher. If you're the person that went to Google, and you're looking specifically for a BMW, and, for some reason, you get an ad that shows the number one position as Mercedes, you feel like, "Man, this search engine sucks. I'm going to go somewhere else."

That's where Google has to make sure that they're serving relevant results, because, at the end of the day, their bread and butter, their revenue, is only going to last as long as they serve relevant results to the people who are searching.

If they're searching and they start to feel like the results are bad, they're going to jump to Bing, or they're going to jump to Yahoo, or some new search engine that comes up down the road.

So Google is hyper-focused on serving relevant results to really retain those eyeballs and to retain that market share within search.

I'm going to talk more specifically about how the AdWords auction process works and what's involved in quality score.

More importantly, how you can leverage that to your advantage to be more relevant than your competition and get a lower cost-per-click.

Why Most Pay-Per-Click Campaigns Fail

Let's talk a little bit about why most pay-per-click campaigns fail. A lot of people I talk to, even more than 50 or 60 percent of the contractors I talk with, tell me that they think pay-per-click advertising is a failed proposition. They spent money. They tried three, four, five different companies. They were never able to get a return on investment.

They really felt like they were pouring money down the drain. This is why most pay-per-click campaigns fail. In most cases, what companies are doing when they set up AdWords for a plumbing or HVAC company is they're setting up one ad group for all of the different services.

If you're Yodle, or if you're ReachLocal, or one of these major companies that's dealing with tens of thousands of clients, then a plumbing company is a relatively simple model.

"OK. You're a plumber, so we're going to bid on 'plumber,' and 'plumbing,' and 'emergency plumber,'

> **If you are set up with just one ad group for all of your services, your relevancy is going to be pretty low.**

and we'll drive them to your home page. You don't even need to have really much of a site. It could just be a one page site. We'll drive leads for you."

But the reality is, within plumbing, there's a lot of different things that you do. The same thing with an HVAC. Within plumbing, you do emergency plumbing, drain cleaning, repiping, bathroom remodeling, garbage disposal repair, septic, and even potentially well work. There is a lot of different searches somebody might type in that can fall into completely different categories.

If you are set up in a way that you just have one ad group for all of your services, your relevancy is going to be pretty low. That makes it so you have to pay more on a per click basis. They don't use specific text ads.

On that same topic, you set up one set of ads. All of those ads have one piece of text in them. It's, "Hey, if you need plumbing services, click here." That's as much thought as went into it. Then when you land on the landing page after you clicked the ad, you get to a very generic page that doesn't have a strong call to action, doesn't have any compelling reason to choose you versus the competition.

You've got a trifecta of failure in the way that a pay-per-click campaign is being structured, if you're down this way. You're not relevant. You don't have a high click through rate because the ad doesn't match up with the keyword. There's no call to action.

Even when they do click on you and you incur that $30 click, they're not impressed. They have no reason to choose you. They hit the back button and they move on. I'm going to explain why this is really the recipe for failure. Remember, highest bid doesn't mean top ranking. Google has to serve the most relevant results. There's a quality score that really drives positioning in cost per click.

- Quality Score

What is this elusive quality score?

In this image here, what I have is the elements that Google has told us are part of their quality score. There's tons of elements at the end of the day, but let's focus on the most important ones:

- Click through rate
- Landing page
- Historical performance of the site
- Various relevancy factors
- Ad relevancy
- Keyword relevancy

What that boils down to is what's your click through rate? Of the people that see your ad, how many of them click on you?

Relevancy, which is if somebody typed in "drain cleaning" or "clogged drain," did they see, "If you've got a clogged drain, click here" or did they see, "Plumbing services. Click here." You can see there's a major difference in relevancy there. Then the quality of the landing page. How fast does the landing page load? Does it match what was written in that text ad?

To the extent that you can get a higher click through rate, be more relevant to the keyword that the person typed in. Have the quality of your landing page match up with the keyword that they typed in. Do this, and you're going to have a higher quality score.

$$\text{ACTUAL CPC} = \frac{\text{AD RANK TO BEAT}}{\text{QUALITY SCORE}} + \$0.01$$

Advertiser	Max. Bid	x	Quality Score	=	(Ad Rank)	Actual CPC
Mary	$2	x	10	=	20 (no. 1)	16/10 + $0.01 = **$1.61**
Tom	$4	x	4	=	16 (no. 2)	

There's a complicated formula which I'm not going to go through in depth here, but the point is, if you've got a better quality score you can pay less on a per click basis while still maintaining the top positions for your keywords.

That's why it's so important that you really understand the way the AdWords auction process works, or at least get this concept that the quality score is important.

If you are relevant, if you have a higher click through rate and your landing page is set up so that it matches what the person typed in, you're going to be able to pay less and still maintain top positioning for your keywords.

Better Quality Score =
Lower Cost Per Click for Top Positions

This is why most pay-per-click campaigns fail. They really ignore the quality score, set up one text ad for all of the services, one ad group, and the landing page isn't compelling. Just as a visual representation, they take all of the logical groupings of keywords, such as "plumbing," "drain cleaning," "bathroom remodeling," and "trenchless sewer replacement."

All they do is take those and they land it on one central page, which is the home page of the website. In my mind, that's really the recipe for failure. That's why more than 50 percent of the people I talk with tell me that pay-per-click is a failed proposition.

Why Most Pay-Per-Click Campaigns Fail

- General Plumbing Services
- Emergency Plumbing
- Water Heater Repair / Replacement
- Drain Cleaning
- Garbage Disposal Repair
- Re-Piping
- Septic Pumping / Cleaning
- Bathroom Remodeling
- Leak Detection
- Trecnhless Sewer Replacement
- Etc, Etc, Etc

YourCompany.com

Getting Great ROI from Pay-Per-Click Marketing

How can you really get this right? How can you maximize the effectiveness of your pay-per-click marketing strategy?

The first thing I recommend is setting up ad groups based on specific services.

I'm going to break those down for you as we go.

- I want you to write a specific and compelling text ad that matches the keywords or those groups of keywords.
- Then I want you to land the traffic that comes through pay-per-click for each ad group on a specific page of the website – not the home page, but a very specific page that matches what they typed in.

If you do this, you can have a better quality score, and you're going to be a lot more successful with your AdWords campaign.

Creating Ad Groups

Within plumbing, what ad groups should you set up? You can go a lot deeper than this. This is just for the sake of getting you to understand what I'm talking about or where I'm going.

General plumbing services: So they typed in "plumber" or "plumbing," "plumbing company," "residential plumber," etc.

All of that can be grouped into a general plumbing services ad group.

Then there's **emergency services**. Somebody is in a much different mental state when they have an emergency. They can be typing, "emergency plumber," "emergency plumbing," "24 hour emergency plumbing services," or "after hours plumber."

For those types of words, you need a different landing page and different text after that. That's a good group if you offer this service.

Other groups could be "water heater installation and repair," "drain cleaning," "garbage disposal repair and installation," "repiping," "septic plumbing and cleaning," "bathroom remodeling," "leak detection," "trenchless sewer replacement," and more.

These are all different classifications or different groups that have different sets of keywords to go along with them. I think it would make sense, assuming you do these services.

You need to think through, "What services do I offer?"

With an HVAC, it's more along the lines of "AC installation," "AC repair," "heating installation," "heating repair," possibly "duct cleaning," and even "indoor air quality."

You want to map out the ad groups that go along with each one of those services. Once you figured out what your ad groups are going to be, then you can start to get specific. How do you set up your ad groups?

- You pick a group of keywords that go with that ad group.
- You write a specific text ad for that ad group.
- Then you land it on a specific page of your website.

Ad Group Templates

Here's the template: Keywords, text ad, landing page. Then you want to think through what the content on that landing page is, because if you're driving traffic to a page that isn't compelling, doesn't have a strong call to action, and there's no reason for them to pick up the phone and call you versus hitting the back button, you're going to start bleeding $15, $20, $30 clicks. Be cognizant of that.

AdGroup: Template

Keywords
- List of Keywords that pertain To that AdGroup

Text Ad
- Should Match The Keyword, Answer the Question and offer a special incentive if possible

Landing Page
Should be mapped to a specific page on you site that speaks to their specific search or need
E.G. www.yoursite.com/city-plumbing-services

Landing Page Content

Are you in need of plumbing services in the Dallas Area? Contact the experts at XYZ Plumbing for immediate, quality & affordable service at 554-555-5533.

Then restate your value proposition, experience, link to reviews, etc

Get $50 Off your service by referencing the coupon below:

COUPON

Call now 554-555-5533.

Ad Group Examples

Let's look at a couple of very specific examples of how you would set this up. The general plumbing ad group could be the keywords like "plumber" or "plumbing," "plumbing service," "plumbing contractor," "your city plumber," "your city plumbing," "best plumbing company," "plumbing companies," and "plumbing contractor."

All of those keywords really fall into the **general plumbing category**.

AdGroup: Plumbing

Keywords
- Plumbing
- Plumbing
- Plumbing Service
- Plumbing Contractor
- CITY plumber, plumbing, etc
- Plumbing Company
- Best Plumbers
- Affordable Plumber
- ETC

Text Ad
- Affordable City Plumber. Get $50 Off!! Same Day Service! Call Now

Landing Page
www.yoursite.com/city-plumbing-services

Landing Page Content

Are you in need of plumbing services in the Dallas Area? Contact the experts at XYZ Plumbing for immediate, quality & affordable service at 554-555-5533.

Then restate your value proposition, experience, link to reviews, etc

Get $50 Off your service by referencing the coupon below:

COUPON

Call now 554-555-5533.

Then you want to write a text ad that's specific to that. Obviously, you're in a specific market, so you would say, "Affordable Dallas Plumber. Get $50 Off. Same Day Service. Call Now." A text ad that's specifically written for that plumbing category.

Then you want to land them on a page of your website, not the home page, but yourcompany.com/plumbing-services. On that page, you want to make sure that you really speak to the psychology of the person based on the keywords that you know they typed in, based on the aggregate you set up.

"Are you in need of plumbing services in the Dallas area? Contact the experts at XYZ Plumbing for immediate quality and affordable service at this number." Restate the value proposition. Talk about why they should choose you; what makes you unique?

Talk about your experience. Let them see reviews. I'm sure you've got online reviews for your company. Showcase those reviews.

Break down the barriers to trust where they can feel like, "OK. This is a quality company. They have good word of mouth about them. They've got a good BBB rating."

Give them the information they need to feel comfortable, and then give them a call to action.

I know not everybody is a fan of coupons and discount rate services. I know we could have a debate about that, and whether that's even a smart thing to do. The reality is, they're online. They're searching for a plumbing service.

There's 20 other people advertising on a pay-per-click basis that they're probably going to have direct click access to within any moment of any day. Give them a reason to choose you versus the competition.

I feel like, "Get $50 off by referencing the coupon below" is one of those ways to say, "This guy's got a coupon. That guy didn't," and get them to call. Give them a strong call to action.

I'm surprised as I audit people's pay-per-click campaigns and see what they have in place, how often you'll get to a landing page, and it's just like, "Hey. We do plumbing. We serve this area," and that's it.

> Give them a reason to choose you versus the competition.

There's no reference to a coupon. There's no reference to online reviews. It doesn't tell them explicitly, "Pick up the phone and call us," or "Click here to schedule your service now."

Make sure they have a call to action, so there's no question they're going to take that next step. That's what I might do within a plumbing ad group.

AdGroup: Emergency

Keywords

- Emergency Plumber
- Emergency Plumbing
- 24 Hour Plumber
- 24 Hr Plumbing Service
- Same Day Plumbing
- After Hours Plumber
- Etc

Text Ad

- Do you have a Plumbing Emergency in Dallas?
  Get Immediate response and...

Landing Page Content

www.yoursite.com/city-emergency-plumbing

Landing Page

Do you have a plumbing emergency in the Dallas Area? Contact the experts at XYZ Plumbing for immediate, quality & affordable service at 554-555-5533.

Then restate your value proposition, experience, link to reviews, etc

Get $50 Off your EMERGENCY service by referencing the coupon below:

COUPON

Call now 554-555-5533.

Emergency. This is different. Keywords to go with an emergency might be, "Emergency Plumber," "Emergency Plumbing," "24 Hour Plumber," "Same Day Plumbing," "After Hours Plumbing," etc.

The text ad, as you can see, needs to be a little bit different. You want to speak to the psychology of those keywords. "Do you have a plumbing emergency in Dallas? Get immediate response and save $50. Call now. Click here."

Then when they get to the page, it should be yourcompany.com/emergency-plumbing. Again, not the home page, not the generic plumbing service page, but the emergency plumbing page.

The content on that page should have a lot of the elements that we talked about. Start with, "Do you have a plumbing emergency? Do you need somebody who can get out to your house today, within the next hour? Click here. Call us today at this phone number."

Restate the value proposition, why they want to choose you. Maybe offer a special discount or incentive. I always encourage you to have video on these pages. It seems silly. Does someone want to see a video when they're in a plumbing emergency? Maybe not, but having a video tends to increase the time on the site.

With an increased time on site, now Google perceives your page to be more relevant, which will enhance your Quality Score.

Same strategies. Talk about what they typed in. Enter the conversation that's happening in their head. Give them very specific compelling reasons they should choose you and take action right now, and then tell them what to do.

AdGroup: Water Heater

Keywords

- Water Heater Repair
- Water Heater
- Water Heaters
- Water Heater Installation
- Water Heater Replacement
- Water Heater Service
- Hot water heaters
- Repair Water Heater
- Etc

Text Ad

- Get Water Heater Repaired in Dallas. Save $50 on your repair! Call Now.

Landing Page

www.yoursite.com/city-water-heater-repair

Landing Page Content

Do you need to repair or replace your water heater in the Dallas Area? Contact the Water Heater Experts at XYZ Plumbing for immediate, quality & affordable service at 554-555-5533.

Then restate your value proposition, experience, link to reviews, etc

Get $50 Off any Water Heater Repair or $75 Off any Replacement

COUPON(S)

Call now 554-555-5533.

Water heaters. This is a totally different thing. "Water Heater Installation," "Water Heater Repair," "Water Heaters," "Hot Water Repair," etc.

You could break water heaters into three separate ad groups if you wanted to. You could have, "Water Heater Installation and Replacement. Water Heater Repair," and then you could have "Tankless Water Heaters" for instance, for those people who are specifically considering tankless.

Write a specific text ad, "Get your water heater repaired in Dallas. Save $50 on your repair. Call now."

Land them on the water heater repair page of the website, and then speak to that conversation. "Do you need to repair or replace your water heater in the Dallas area? Contact the water heater experts at XYZ Plumbing for immediate quality affordable service."

This is boiler plate type stuff. Be creative. Make sure you stand out from the competition, but the concept remains. Enter the conversation based on what they typed in.

Speak to the specific reasons they would want to choose you versus the competition.

AdGroup: Drain Cleaning

Keywords
- Clogged Drain
- Drain Cleaning
- Drain Clearing
- Blocked Drain
- Drain Cleaning Service
- Rooter Service
- Drain Snaking
- Etc

Text Ad
- Clogged Drain in Dallas. Call The Drain Experts. Save $50 on your repair! Call Now.

Landing Page
www.yoursite.com/city-drain-cleaning-service

Landing Page Content

Do you have a clogged or blocked drain in the Dallas Area? Contact the Drain Cleaning & Rooter Experts at XYZ Plumbing for immediate, quality & affordable service at 554-555-5533.

Then restate your value proposition, experience, link to reviews, etc

Get $50 Off any Drain Cleaning Repair

COUPON(S)

Call now 554-555-5533.

Drain Cleaning. This is a whole category in and of itself. It might be "Clogged Drain." It might be "Drain Clearing." It might be "Blocked Drain." It might be "Rooter Service." It might be "Drain Snaking."

These are keywords to indicate they've got a clog, and they need somebody to come out and unclog it.

You would write something like, "Clogged drain in Dallas? Call the drain experts. Save $50 on your repair. Call now." Land them on the drain cleaning page of your website.

Then talk to that conversation. "Do you have a clogged or blocked drain in the Dallas area? Contact the drain experts." Restate the value. Show them the reviews. Give them an offer, a special incentive to take action now!

I prepared this in a way that I wanted to really hammer on the concept.

- Set up your ad groups.
- Pick your keywords.
- Write a specific text ad.
- Set up a landing page. Make sure the content on that landing page resonates with the customer and answers the specific questions that they're asking.

AdGroup: Bathroom Remodeling

Keywords

- Bathroom Remodeling
- Bathroom Renovation
- Bathroom Contractor
- Bathroom Remodeling Contractor
- Remodel Bathroom
- Etc

Text Ad

- Thinking or remodeling your Bath in Dallas? Get a FREE estimate today.

Landing Page

www.yoursite.com/city-bathroom-remodeling

Landing Page Content

Are you thinking of remodeling or renovating your bathroom in the City Area? Contact the Experts at XYZ Plumbing for quality, affordable bathroom remodeling services.

Then restate your value proposition, experience, link to reviews, etc

Offer A FREE Ideas Guide in exchange for name / eMail Address.

LEAD CAPTURE FORM
Call now 554-555-5533 for a free estimate.

We'll just do one more example. This example could really apply to **bathroom remodeling**. It could apply to repiping. It could apply to trench lists. These are higher transaction value services, where there's probably a little bit longer of a sales cycle.

If they've got a plumbing emergency – they typed in "Emergency plumber" and they get to your page – they're pretty much going to pick up the phone and take action right then and there.

With the higher transaction services where they know they could be spending $10,000, $20,000, $30,000, they might spend a little bit more time, researching it – making sure that they make the right decision, making sure that they choose the right company on getting bids.

What you want to do that's a little bit different on these pages is to make sure you have some type of lead capture mechanism that's more than just, "Call us today."

On our template, we've got our keywords and we've got the text, "Thinking of remodeling your bath in Dallas? Get a free estimate today." So you want to land them on that specific page of the website and when you talk to them on the page have something like, "Are you thinking about remodeling or renovating?" then give them the information.

Explain why they would want to choose you versus the competition, but then offer them some type of lead capture mechanism. This is just "Download Our Bathroom Remodeling Style Guide." If they're thinking about remodeling a bathroom, then maybe they want to get some additional information and get ideas.

Offer them a guide of some sort, and it doesn't have to be long – it could be like a little five pager with pictures of different types of bathrooms. If they are interested, they will enter their name and email address in order to get that guide."

> If you follow these strategies, your return on investment is going to be significantly greater.

Now you've got their email information, and you can email them over a predefined period of time.

Maybe set up six emails over the next 30 days, where they're going to get an email from you every few days with new information, such as, "Hey! Just wanted to touch base. I know you were considering remodeling your bathroom. We recently completed a project in the Dallas area and wanted to show you some of the befores and afters."

Boom! Now, they're like, "That's really cool! I'm really appreciating that they sent this. I was still thinking about doing my bathroom." You can remain top of mind with them over an extended period of time.

That really improves your probability of getting those higher transaction sales by collecting names and email addresses from those folks specifically, and dripping information to them over time.

I really feel like if you do this correctly, if you follow these strategies, or at least you take these strategies to your current provider and say, "I want to make sure I break it into these six or seven categories, and that we've got intelligently structured text ads and landing pages," your return on investment is going to be significantly greater.

There's no way it wouldn't be. You're going to be getting a lower cost per click, because your relevancy is higher.

Then you're going to get a better conversion from click to call, or click to lead, because your landing page is speaking to the person's situation, which is really what they want. They want an answer to a problem.

Best Practices for Setting Up Your AdWords Campaign

- Local Extensions

One of the things I recommend is setting up a location extension within your ad group campaign, or AdWords campaign. What that does is it takes your AdWords campaign and it connects it with your Google Maps listing.

Setup your Location Extensions
(Google Map Listing)

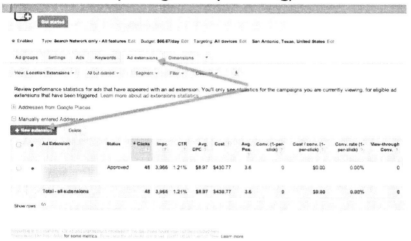

It's as simple as within AdWords clicking "Ad Extensions" and choosing a local extension.

Doing this makes it so that when your ad shows up, not only does your text ad show up, but also a little map marker and your address, which is great for plumbing and HVAC related services. It gives you more real estate on the page.

You're taking up a bigger block of space than the competition, and your client wants to know they're dealing with somebody local and not some national chain. When they see, "OK. Look at where they're located," that helps with your click through rate and with your conversion rate.

I always like to connect that with local extensions.

- Importance of Testing

The other thing you want to do is always make sure that you're split testing your ads. I talked about Quality Score and click through rate being a very high factor in that quality score.

Click through rate means if 100 people see your ad, and let's say only 10 people click on it, that's a 10 percent click through rate. If you can bump that 10 percent to 15 percent, Google will say, "Wow! This is a really relevant ad."

Ad	Ad group	Labels	Status	% Served	Clicks	Impr.	CTR	Avg. CPC
Total - all campaign					58	5,275	1.10%	$9.43
Bathtub Installation Pros Local Bathtub Installers. Call To Schedule an Appointment	*R - Bathtub Installation	–	Approved	0.97%	1	51	1.96%	$3.71
Bathtub Plumbing Repair Need your Bathtub Repaired? Call Now to Get an Estimate	*R - Bathtub Plumbing Service & Repair	–	Approved	1.08%	0	57	0.00%	$0.00
Drain Cleaning & Clogs Drain Clog Removal Experts. Fast, Same Day & 24/7 Service	*R - Drain Cleaning & Clogs	–	Approved	0.83%	6	44	13.64%	$10.05
Drain Installation Pros Local Drain Installation Service. Call To Schedule an Appointment	*R - Drain Installation	–	Approved	0.95%	1	50	2.00%	$9.51

What you want to do is within each one of your ad groups, such as the plumbing ad group and the emergency plumbing ad group; make sure that you have two versions of your ad.

Review it at the end of the month and see which one had the higher click through rate.

What you can do over time is start to develop a control. You might have one ad that converts at 13 percent. You'll keep running split tests against that ad every single month until something gets a 14 percent click through rate. Then you say, "The control is gone and now this is our control." By doing that on a consistent basis for each one of your ad groups, that's how you can get a better click through rate, and a better quality score, and continue to get a lower cost per click over time for your keywords on your AdWords campaign.

- Monitor Page Position

The other thing I'd like to make sure you're paying attention to is your average position on the page. When we run a search in Google, again it's the area on the top in the right hand corner that is your pay-per-click listings.

The further down the right hand column that you go, the lower the probability that the person that clicks on you is going to be a good quality person.

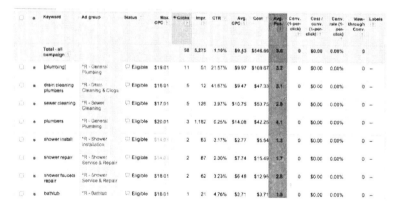

If you're bidding so low that you're all the way down at the very bottom of the right-hand side, your click through rate is going to be skewed against you. Most people aren't looking in that area. They're looking at the top one on the left, and maybe the one on the top right-hand corner, and so your click through rate is lower. Your Quality Score is lower. It starts to really create a vicious cycle, where you're really not going to get the amount of clicks that you should for the right cost per click, and so pay attention.

In the example above, I've got a couple of check marks and a couple of "X" marks.

The way that Google AdWords scores this is that the first one is one, the second one is two, the next one is three, and then the first one in the top right-hand corner is four.

I'm going to recommend you try and average between a one and four position.

If you start to see yourself averaging five, six, seven, then you're going to have a tough time really making this work well for you.

AdWords Best Practices

● Pay Attention to Exact Match vs. Broad Match

● Add Negative Keywords where appropriate to protect your budget

★ Jobs, Employment, Marketing,etc

- Keyword Match

Also, you want to pay attention to the distinction between "exact" match and "broad" match. Exact match is somebody goes in and they type in "Emergency plumber," and you're bidding on that keyword.

Broad match would mean any version of that keyword that somebody might type in.

Let's say they typed in "Emergency plumbing jobs," or "Emergency plumbing article" – things that really weren't what you had in mind, and they don't really have the same commercial intent.

If you're doing broad match, Google says, "Anything that contains 'emergency plumbing' in it is a good fit," and that's not necessarily the case. You want to pay attention to that. There are ways to structure it correctly.

If you're doing this on your own, or you don't feel like you're very sophisticated and don't really know, I would recommend getting a little more specific with exact match, choosing the exact keywords the way that you want them, and spend some time doing it this way.

The other thing you want to do is to add some logical negative keywords. As an example, "Jobs," "Marketing," "Article," "How Tos," or things you want to negate.

The reason for that is let's say somebody types in "Dallas plumbing," that's a great turn. "Dallas plumbing jobs," that's somebody looking for a job within your plumbing company or within any plumbing company. A keyword like "Dallas plumbing" is a very high cost per click word. We could be looking at $25 per click for that type of keyword, maybe more.

It's OK. You can make that work for somebody that's actually looking for plumbing services, but you don't want to be spending $25 per click for a random plumber that's looking for a job in Dallas.

That's where you can put in negatives like Jobs, Employment, Careers, Marketing, Plumbing Marketing, How to Articles. Negate those words and then you avoid paying unnecessarily for keywords that don't add any value to your paid marketing campaign.

- Mobile Devices

The next thing you want to do is we talked about the fact that more and more people are getting to your plumbing website via mobile devices, and especially if we're thinking about emergency plumbing services, emergency A/C repair services.

It's much easier to pull out your phone and run that "Dallas plumber" search, than it is to pull it up on your desktop and run a search.

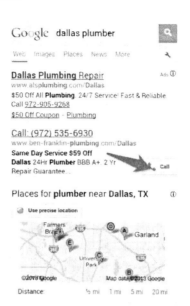

What we're finding is with the way Google pay-per-click is working on most mobile devices, and we're talking about iPhones and Android phones, the paid listings take up almost 50 percent of the real estate.

The people would have to really scroll down in order to see organic listings.

I talked about the importance of having pay-per-click advertising as part of your overall online marketing strategy; with a lot more traffic coming via mobile, if you don't have a paid ad, you could be missing those opportunities.

The other thing you can do that's really neat within mobile pay-per-click is you can set up a call extension.

When they see your ad, they can just hit that "Call" button, and the arrow is pointing to it on the screen. Rather than visiting your website, and kind of browsing around and trying to find your phone number, they will literally just be calling your office. It's a little click to call in that case.

The way that you set that up is through a specific mobile campaign. You want to select that as the campaign type, "Mobile Devices Only." Pick your Geo location, whatever your

124

> You want to pay close attention to your metrics like your cost per call and your average sale transaction

service area is, and then turn on the "Click To Call" function. That's how you're able to get it set up with something like this.

The cost per click on mobile is significantly higher. You want to pay close attention to your metrics as far as what your cost per call is, and what your average sale transaction is.

If you know your numbers well, then you can play this game. You can get those mobile searchers.

If they're searching on a mobile device, they're probably in action mode.

They need someone to come out immediately. They're not kicking tires.

It's worth it in my mind if you know your numbers to really play aggressively on the mobile side of the equation.

Know Your Metrics

- Budgets

Some other things you want to pay attention to with your AdWords campaign is that a decent budget within a plumbing or HVAC company is probably going to be no less than $1,500 per month.

We have clients that we deal with that spend in the $15,000 to $20,000 per month range. The spread on this is pretty significant.

As long as you know your numbers, and you've got the right tracking mechanisms in place, it's almost like going to a slot machine and putting in $1 and getting a $5 bill out.

If you can consistently set up your pay-per-click campaign where you're putting in $1 and $5 comes out, if you've got the manpower and you've got the scalability in your business, why wouldn't you scale it to $10,000 or $15,000 per month? It just makes sense.

> As long as you know your numbers, it's almost like putting $1 into a slot machine and getting $5 out.

You should not do that until you know your metrics, and you're really clear on, "Am I putting in a dollar and getting a dollar back? If so, does that work for me? Am I putting a dollar and getting two dollars back?" Or in most cases, we hate to see this, putting a dollar in and get like 10 cents back.

That is a good way to bankrupt the company. You want to make sure you know your metrics.

- Google Analytics

Some of the metrics you want to look at first is Google Analytics. Google Analytics will just tell you how many people are getting to the website and what they typed in to get there.

You can start to search and see how many came in via paid versus organic. You can see how much time they are spending on the site. You can see what your bounce rate is. It's important to watch the analytics and make sure the number is working in a good direction.

- Call Tracking

The other thing you want to put in place is called "Call Tracking." There's tools out there that I recommend.

The one we use is called "CallRail." There's also Call Flyer, CallSource, Mongoose Metrics and there's lots of these services out there.

What we happen to like really well about CallRail is that you can set up a code on your website that allows you to swap so that if somebody gets to the website organically, they see an organic tracking number, an SEO tracking number.

If they get to the website via pay-per-click, it passes the information through to the website. The website says, "This is a pay-per-click visitor." Then the visitor sees a pay-per-click tracking number when they get to the website.

This gives you the ability to really start to isolate how many calls did we get from the pay-per-click activity specifically, and hear recordings of those conversations, and really start to quantify, "Well, I got 77 inbound calls directly from pay-per-click, and I spent $2,000."

Play back the recordings and see how many of those calls turn into a booked service, then you start to figure out what those metrics are. "Am I putting in a dollar and getting three dollars back? Can I live with that within my business?" If so, then you can start to scale the budget as it makes financial sense.

> I really don't recommend running pay-per-click in the absence of the right type of tracking.

There's a lot of systems that do this now. I really don't recommend running pay-per-click in the absence of this type of tracking, where you can see how many calls came in directly from pay-per-click. Same on the organics, how many calls came directly from the non pay-per-click listings.

Summary

Just to recap what we've covered, you can really succeed within pay-per-click if you set up your AdWords in a way that positions you for success.

You do that by setting up ad groups based on keywords, setting up very specific text ads and then landing traffic on specific pages of your website.

The reason for that is, as your relevancy improves, your cost per click will decline and your conversion rate will increase.

What that means is you're going to get a better return on the overall investment that you're making in your pay-per-click marketing campaign. I hope you got a lot of value out of this. I hope it gives you a new perspective on pay-per-click advertising and what you could do within your online marketing strategy.

I've developed a little checklist that goes along with this. It walks you through what you need to do step by step to make sure that you're maximizing your potential and you're structuring your campaign correctly.

If you want to download the checklist you can go to plumberseo.net/ppcchecklist.

Joshua D. Nelson

#10: Do you have proper tracking in place to gauge your ROI?

The final item on our checklist asks, "Do you have the proper tools in place to track your return on investment?"

It's really easy with all the things we've talked about to spend a lot of money, to spend a lot of time, and not get a return.

- At the end of the day, this is not about better rankings.
- It's not about more visitors.
- It's about more calls, turning into more revenue, which falls to your bottom line.

You want to make sure that you spend some time really putting the right tools in place to track and measure your progress.

There are three main tools I recommend you put in place.

> ## Google Analytics

The first tool is Google Analytics.

This lets you run important reports like how many people got to your website this week, how many people got to your website this month and in the last three months.

What it will tell you is whether the number of visitors getting to your website is increasing.

If you're implementing the strategies I've outlined here, the number of visitors should be increasing.

> ## Keyword Tracking

The other thing I want to encourage you to put in place is keyword tracking. We talked at the beginning about selecting your keywords, and trying to figure out where you're ranking on the search engines – plumber, plumbing, emergency plumber, drain cleaning, etc.

There are tools – like BrightLocal, SEO Book, Raven Tools, where you can put your list online and have a report run on a weekly basis, a monthly basis or a quarterly basis – that will show you exactly where you rank on Google and Yahoo and Bing for those keywords.

I encourage you to put that type of tracking in place.

> ## Call Tracking

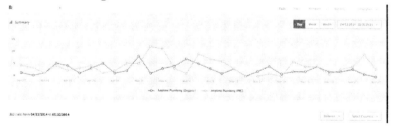

The third critical tracking element, probably the most important, is call tracking. I really want to encourage you to put call tracking on your website, primarily in places that aren't going to interfere with your name, address and phone number consistency for the Google Maps.

That will allow you to really gauge how many calls came in this month, next month, the month after, and so on. That's going to be the true measure of, are you getting a return on investment, especially if you use a call service like CallRail or CallFire.

That allows you to hear the recordings of those conversations and quantify – for example, that you got 72 inbound calls, but:

- o   What happened with those calls?
- o   Were they good leads?
- o   Did they turn into booked revenue?

Those are the call tracking mechanisms I want to encourage you to put in place.

Another option is some type of CRM where you're tracking your lead sources, so that you can really know, "Well, we spent $2,500 in online marketing, but we got $32,000 in revenue".

That's going to be the real metric that helps you gauge the true return on investment.

Those are the key tracking mechanisms I want to encourage you to put in place.

BUILDING A PLAN AND LEARNING FROM OTHERS

So, now that you've gotten this far, how are you doing?

We worked all of the way through the worksheet. I'm hoping at this point you've got some things circled, you've got some things highlighted, and you're starting to realize, here's what I need to do right away.

You should have identified some things you need to take action on and start to build a plan of action to double, triple, or even 10x your sales within your business.

I want to encourage you that this stuff works. I want to show you some additional case studies of how this has played out for other plumbing and HVAC companies.

One of the companies that we work with is Schuler Services out of Allentown, Pennsylvania.

When we started working with them, the owner Greg Joyce had just bought the business from his dad. He'd worked as a trade plumber within the company for pretty much his entire life.

This is a second generation company, a sizable company in their market. They do about $2 million per year. They're not a small company by any stretch of the imagination.

Similar to The Plumbing Doctor, they had built their business in the Yellow Pages. Heavy Yellow Page ads worked really well over the years but it wasn't working as well into the mid-2000s.

Greg, as he took over the company, decided he needed to put a really aggressive plan in place because he wants to make some money with this business he just bought from his dad.

He connected with us, and we implemented the plan that I've outlined throughout the course of this book.

You can see, if we go to Allentown plumber, within a matter of four or five months, they now hold the dominant position in their market for Allentown plumber, Allentown plumbing, Allentown drain cleaning, and a lot of the other keywords.

At the same time, traffic to the website has shown a significant increase from 477 visitors to 863 visitors.

The big metric here that made a huge impact, was their website was very basic.

It was just not very good. We went and we infused personality into the website.

We started showcasing the reviews. We put the pictures of the trucks and the team; it tapped into their brand, where they've been in that market for quite some time.

The numbers took a significant jump, from 42 calls to 121 calls.

Here's what Greg Joyce had to say, "We're currently up 40 percent year over year, and busier than ever."

We're talking about a $2 million per year company that is up 40 percent, that's $800,000 in increased revenue as a result of getting their Internet marketing right, in a small town like Allentown, Pennsylvania.

I want to encourage you that these same strategies and techniques can work in your market, and they will have a major impact on your bottom line.

Another case study I can share was how Shamrock Plumbing got 319 calls from the Internet in April.

When we started with Shamrock Plumbing, he was a one man operation working from a home office, and really just struggling to get his business off the ground.

He's been with us for several years now and it's been an interactive process.

We really were able to implement this entire process. We got his website right, made sure it was optimized correctly for all of his different cities and all of the different services that he provides.

There is a heavy emphasis on repiping in his market and a heavy emphasis on drain cleaning.

We really were able to move him up in the search engines.

What happened was, over this period of three to four years, he went from a one man operation to a six man operation working out of a 2500 square foot office there in central Florida, in Orlando.

Of course if we run a search right now for Orlando plumber, Orlando plumbing, Orlando drain cleaning, and Orlando water heater repair, he holds a very dominant position.

It's all a function of the exact strategies I've outlined here and that are in your worksheet.

If we look just at the period of time, between 2012 and 2014, he went from 250 visitors to 893 visitors. What that meant was it increased from 25 calls to 113 calls in January and in April it was 319 calls directly via the web.

I just want you to think for a second, what an increase to 319 inbound calls and leads would mean to your business.

As we come to the close of this book, I want you to review your "Get Your Internet Marketing Right Checklist" and evaluate.

- Do you have these strategies being implemented correctly in your company?
- Do you have the resources to get this done on your own?
- Do you have somebody either on your team or outside your team that you can work with to implement these strategies to take your company to the next level?

If you can answer yes to all of these questions, you are well positioned to take your business to the next level. I hope you've found this book useful and will keep me posted on your success.

If you answer no to any of them, I'd love to work with you to help you get your Internet marketing right.

Please join me on the next page and I'll tell you more.

NEXT STEPS

Here's the process I would like to follow if you're interested in having me help you implement these strategies in your company.

Keyword Research

The first thing I want to do is I want to help develop your keyword list. It all starts with understanding what keywords people are typing in when they need your services.

The first thing I'm going to do is I'm going to do some research based on your service, based on the cities that you operate in and develop a keyword list for you.

From there, we're going to determine your rankings. How are you ranking for those keywords on Google, Yahoo, Bing – both the organic and Map listings – That will help us figure out where we're at, where we start and where we need to improve.

Conversion

We'll look at the conversion elements on your website. Is your current website up to snuff or does it need to be revised? Does it need more personality? Does it need a stronger call to action on certain pages in the website? We're going to review those conversion elements and then we're going to look at the off page factors.

Authority

Do you have enough links? Do you have bad links? Do you have your citations with the right consistency? Do you have online reviews? Do you have a process in place to get real reviews from real customers and your true service area?

Plan of Action

We're going to develop a recommended course of action – what needs to be done based on where you're at today to potentially double, triple or 10x your sales over the next six to nine months.

Now, my time is valuable. My team's time is valuable. Putting together this report for you takes time, explaining what the report means takes time and I value that time at about $349.

I think it would be a steal for you to pay me $349 to put this assessment together for you.

However, you've made the commitment to invest in my book and you've invested the time to read it and I appreciate that. I appreciate the opportunity to share great ideas and strategies with you.

So I'm not going to charge you $349, I'm just asking for a courtesy deposit of $50. That $50 tells me that you're serious so that:

- If my team and I take the time to do this research for you, you're going to show up for the call.
- If what we show you is compelling, you're serious about potentially hiring us to do this for you and really take your Internet marketing strategy and run with it on your behalf – like we did for Shamrock Plumbing and The Plumbing Doctor and hundreds of other plumbing companies throughout the United States.

Now, as a special bonus for taking action on this, I'm going to send you a CD / DVD program that I developed.

It's called "Your Plumbing & HVAC Online Marketing Plan" and it's about an hour and a half long, with more in depth detail on some of the topics which we covered in this book.

This training CD / DVD program will be mailed to your office included for just that $50 deposit.

If you want to take me up on this offer, there's two things you can do.

- The first and easiest would be to call us. Call us at 866-610-4647 we'd love to talk with you, brainstorm a little bit and get this off the ground for you.

Or, if you prefer:

- You can go to http://www.plumberseo.net/apply-now and enter your contact information and we'll get back to you and schedule the assessment and do our research.

Now, I do need to tell you that we only work with one plumbing or HVAC company in each market. So, if you're in one of the markets where we have a client currently, unfortunately we won't be able to work with you.

With that said, I encourage you to follow up on this immediately.

If you are serious about getting your Internet marketing right and you'd like to have our team implement this for you, give us a call right now at **866-610-4647** or go to http://www.plumberseo.net/apply-now

APPENDICES

GET YOUR ONLINE MARKETING RIGHT: WORKSHEET

Check off the things you are doing and circle those you are not.

- Do you have a website?

- How many phone calls are you getting each month from your website?

- Is it properly optimized for search?
    - Do you have your main keyword on the Title Tag on each of the pages of your website? e.g. Your City Plumber | Your Company Name
    - Do you have pages for each of your core services?
    - Do you have pages for the brands that you service?
    - Do you have unique content on each of the pages of your website?
    - Are you helping Google understand your true service area?

- Does your website rank on page one when customers type, "your city HVAC contractor", "your city heating repair", "your city ac repair" and other similar keywords?

- Is your website optimized for conversion (visitors to callers)?
    - Do you have the Phone Number in the top right-hand corner on every page?
    - Are you using authentic images / video? Photo of the owner, photo of your trucks, photo of your office, photo of your team, etc.?
    - Do you have a compelling Call to Action after every blog of text?

- Is your website MOBILE site-friendly?

- Are you consistently creating new content, blogging and creating new inbound links back to your website?

- Have you optimized correctly for the Google Map Listings
    - What is your Google Login for Google Plus & Google Places?

- o Have you properly optimized your listing?
- o Are you on all the major online directory listings with the same company name, address & phone number?
- o How many online reviews do you have?
- o Do you have a proactive strategy for getting new online reviews every day?

- Are you active on Social Media?
  - o Do you have your business profiles setup on Facebook, Twitter, Google+, LinkedIn, and YouTube?
  - o How many likes do you have on Facebook?
  - o Are you updating your social profiles on a daily basis?

- Are you leveraging Email Marketing?
  - o Do you have a database with your customer email addresses?
  - o Are you sending out a monthly email newsletter?
  - o Are you leveraging email to get online reviews & to draw customers into your social media profiles?

- Are you taking advantage of paid online marketing opportunities?
  - o Do you have an AdWords Campaign? Are you strategically targeting with specific ad groups, text ads & landing pages?
  - o Do you have a premium ad on Angie's List, Yelp, CitySearch, YP.com?
  - o Are you taking advantage of Paid Lead Services - Home Advisor, etc.?

- Do you have the proper tracking in place to gauge your ROI?
  - o Google Analytics
  - o Keyword Ranking Tracking
  - o Call Tracking
  - o CRM with tracked lead sources

DOWNLOAD THE WORKSHEET AT
HTTP://WWW.PLUMBERSEO.NET/HANDOUT

KEYWORDS – PLUMBING

Keyword	Monthly Search Volume	Keywords You Want To Focus On
plumber	74,000	Your City + plumber
plumbing	60,500	Your City + plumbing
water filtration systems	9,900	Your City + water filtration systems
clogged toilet	9,900	Your City + clogged toilet
bathroom remodeling	8,100	Your City + bathroom remodeling
tankless water heaters	6,600	Your City + tankless water heaters
garbage disposal repair	6,600	Your City + garbage disposal repair
leak detection	6,600	Your City + leak detection
drain cleaning	5,400	Your City + drain cleaning
water heater repair	5,400	Your City + water heater repair
septic tank cleaning	5,400	Your City + septic tank cleaning
water softener systems	4,400	Your City + water softener systems
emergency plumber	4,400	Your City + emergency plumber
water heater installation	4,400	Your City + water heater installation
boiler repair	4,400	Your City + boiler repair
boiler replacement	4,400	Your City + boiler replacement
sewer cleaning	2,900	Your City + sewer cleaning
septic pumping	2,900	Your City + septic pumping
toilet installation	2,400	Your City + toilet installation
water heater replacement	2,400	Your City + water heater replacement
septic cleaning	1,900	Your City + septic cleaning
emergency plumbing	1,900	Your City + emergency plumbing

tankless water heater installation	1,900	Your City + tankless water heater installation
shower installation	1,900	Your City + shower installation
plumbing service	1,300	Your City + plumbing service
backflow testing	1,300	Your City + backflow testing
gas line installation	1,000	Your City + gas line installation
plumbing contractor	880	Your City + plumbing contractor
sewer repair	880	Your City + sewer repair
pipe lining	880	Your City + pipe lining
sump pump repair	720	Your City + sump pump repair
garbage disposal replacement	590	Your City + garbage disposal replacement
backflow certification	590	Your City + backflow certification
sewer line replacement	590	Your City + sewer line replacement
commercial plumber	480	Your City + commercial plumber
rooter service	480	Your City + rooter service
gas line repair	480	Your City + gas line repair
repiping	390	Your City + repiping
slab leak repair	390	Your City + slab leak repair
24 hour plumbing service	320	Your City + 24 hour plumbing service
tub installation	320	Your City + tub installation
hydrojetting	260	Your City + hydrojetting
burst pipe repair	210	Your City + burst pipe repair
sewer line inspection	140	Your City + sewer line inspection
trenchless sewer replacement	110	Your City + trenchless sewer replacement
clogged toilet repair	110	Your City + clogged toilet repair
backflow repair	90	Your City + backflow repair
sewer pumping	50	Your City + sewer pumping

septic plumbing	70	Your City + septic plumbing
commercial plumbing contractor	50	Your City + commercial plumbing contractor
water softener system installation	50	Your City + water softener system installation
sewer cleanouts	30	Your City + sewer cleanouts
leak location	40	Your City + leak location
video sewer line inspection	20	Your City + video sewer line inspection
water filtration system installation	20	Your City + water filtration system installation

Download the plumbing keyword list at
http://www.plumberseo.net/plumbing-keywords

KEYWORDS – HVAC

Keyword	Monthly Search Volume	Page You Want To Optimize For
air conditioning	16,600,000	Your City + air conditioning
air conditioner	13,600,000	Your City + air conditioner
ac air conditioning	9,140,000	Your City + ac air conditioning
furnace	5,000,000	Your City + furnace
air conditioners	3,350,000	Your City + air conditioners
hvac	1,830,000	Your City + hvac
air condition	1,500,000	Your City + air condition
Trane	1,220,000	Your City + trane
hvac air conditioning	1,000,000	Your City + hvac air conditioning
heat pump	823,000	Your City + heat pump
heating air	823,000	Your City + heating air
heating & air	823,000	Your City + heating & air
heating and air	823,000	Your City + heating and air
air conditioning units	823,000	Your City + air conditioning units
air conditioning unit	823,000	Your City + air conditioning unit
air conditioner unit	673,000	Your City + air conditioner unit
air conditioner units	673,000	Your City + air conditioner units
heating & cooling	673,000	Your City + heating & cooling
cooling and heating	673,000	Your City + cooling and heating

heating and cooling	673,000	Your City + heating and cooling
air conditioning cooling	673,000	Your City + air conditioning cooling
heat and air	550,000	Your City + heat and air
air conditioning and heating	550,000	Your City + air conditioning and heating
heating and air conditioning	550,000	Your City + heating and air conditioning
heating air conditioning	550,000	Your City + heating air conditioning
heating & air conditioning	550,000	Your City + heating & air conditioning
air conditioning heating	550,000	Your City + air conditioning heating
portable air conditioner	450,000	Your City + portable air conditioner
air conditioner portable	450,000	Your City + air conditioner portable
central air	368,000	Your City + central air
portable air conditioning	368,000	Your City + portable air conditioning
air conditioning portable	368,000	Your City + air conditioning portable
portable air conditioners	368,000	Your City + portable air conditioners
air conditioners portable	368,000	Your City + air conditioners portable
air conditioning system	368,000	Your City + air conditioning system
air conditioning repair	301,000	Your City + air conditioning repair
repair air conditioning	301,000	Your City + repair air conditioning
air conditioner price	301,000	Your City + air conditioner price

window air conditioner	301,000	Your City + window air conditioner
air conditioner repair	246,000	Your City + air conditioner repair
portable air conditioning units	246,000	Your City + portable air conditioning units
repair air conditioner	246,000	Your City + repair air conditioner
air conditioning systems	246,000	Your City + air conditioning systems
air conditioner system	246,000	Your City + air conditioner system
portable air conditioning unit	246,000	Your City + portable air conditioning unit
ac compressor	246,000	Your City + ac compressor
split air conditioner	246,000	Your City + split air conditioner
duct cleaning	201,000	Your City + duct cleaning
air conditioning price	201,000	Your City + air conditioning price
ac unit	201,000	Your City + ac unit
air conditioner prices	201,000	Your City + air conditioner prices
window air conditioning	201,000	Your City + window air conditioning
window air conditioners	201,000	Your City + window air conditioners
air conditioning service	201,000	Your City + air conditioning service
service air conditioning	201,000	Your City + service air conditioning
cost air conditioner	201,000	Your City + cost air conditioner
air conditioner cost	201,000	Your City + air conditioner cost

ac repair	165,000	Your City + ac repair
cost of air conditioning	165,000	Your City + cost of air conditioning
air conditioning cost	165,000	Your City + air conditioning cost
air conditioning compressor	165,000	Your City + air conditioning compressor
air conditioning prices	165,000	Your City + air conditioning prices
heater repair	165,000	Your City + heater repair
air conditioner systems	165,000	Your City + air conditioner systems
air conditioners price	165,000	Your City + air conditioners price
air conditions	165,000	Your City + air conditions
ac units	165,000	Your City + ac units
air conditioner service	165,000	Your City + air conditioner service
service air conditioner	165,000	Your City + service air conditioner
air conditioning equipment	165,000	Your City + air conditioning equipment
split air conditioners	165,000	Your City + split air conditioners
hvac heating	165,000	Your City + hvac heating
furnace parts	165,000	Your City + furnace parts
ac service	135,000	Your City + ac service
central air conditioning	135,000	Your City + central air conditioning

LG air conditioner	135,000	Your City + LG air conditioner
central air conditioner	135,000	Your City + central air conditioner
service ac	135,000	Your City + service ac
window unit air conditioner	135,000	Your City + window unit air conditioner
window air conditioning units	135,000	Your City + window air conditioning units
air conditioning window units	135,000	Your City + air conditioning window units
air conditioners prices	135,000	Your City + air conditioners prices
auto air conditioning	135,000	Your City + auto air conditioning
air conditioner reviews	135,000	Your City + air conditioner reviews
vent cleaning	110,000	Your City + vent cleaning
furnace repair	110,000	Your City + furnace repair
air conditioning parts	110,000	Your City + air conditioning parts
central air conditioners	110,000	Your City + central air conditioners
air conditioning services	110,000	Your City + air conditioning services
home air conditioning	110,000	Your City + home air conditioning
air conditioning home	110,000	Your City + air conditioning home
LG air conditioning	110,000	Your City + LG air conditioning
split air conditioning	110,000	Your City + split air conditioning

fix air conditioning	110,000	Your City + fix air conditioning
LG air conditioners	110,000	Your City + LG air conditioners
fix air conditioner	110,000	Your City + fix air conditioner
air condition units	110,000	Your City + air condition units
air conditioners reviews	110,000	Your City + air conditioners reviews
air conditioning servicing	110,000	Your City + air conditioning servicing
air conditioner servicing	110,000	Your City + air conditioner servicing
servicing air conditioner	110,000	Your City + servicing air conditioner
home air conditioner	110,000	Your City + home air conditioner
air conditioner home	110,000	Your City + air conditioner home
air duct cleaning	90,500	Your City + air duct cleaning
air conditioner installation	60,500	Your City + air conditioner installation
air conditioning installation	60,500	Your City + air conditioning installation
air conditioning contractor	40,500	Your City + air conditioning contractor
hvac contractor	33,100	Your City + hvac contractor
heating contractor	33,100	Your City + heating contractor
ac installation	27,100	Your City + ac installation

ac repair service	22,200	Your City + ac repair service
air conditioner contractor	9,900	Your City + air conditioner contractor
ac contractor	5,400	Your City + ac contractor
ac repair contractor	1,300	Your City + ac repair contractor
ac installation service	260	Your City + ac installation service
ac installation contractor	-	Your City + ac installation contractor
a/c repair	-	Your City + a/c repair
a/c contractor	-	Your City + a/c contractor
a/c service	-	Your City + a/c service
a/c repair service	-	Your City + a/c repair service
a/c installation contractor	-	Your City + a/c installation contractor
a/c installation service	-	Your City + a/c installation service

Download the Heating & Cooling keyword list at
http://www.hvacseo.net/keywords

Schedule your Assessment & Strategy Session Now

Here's Everything You Get...

- **Your Custom Keyword List** – based on your services, service area & search trends. We know the most searched plumbing & HVAC services ($197 value)
- **Ranking Report** – Showing exactly where your company currently ranks online for those essential keywords ($97 value)
- **Website Optimization Review** – We will explain exactly why your website is not ranking currently and what needs to be done to bridge the gap ($97 value)
- **Website Conversion Review** – We will point out the little things that could be preventing your website from converting visitors to callers / leads ($97 value)
- **Our "Your Internet Marketing" CD / DVD Training** – We will mail you our CD / DVD training program outlining your Online Marketing Plan ($47 Value)
- **Your Plan for "Getting your Online Marketing Right"** – Outlines exactly what needs to be done in your unique situation going forward to fully leverage the internet for more calls, leads & profits in your plumbing or HVAC business ($197 value)

Total Value: $349
Today Just $50

If you want to take me up on this offer, there's two things you can do.

- The first and easiest would be to call us. Call us at **866-610-4647**; we'd love to talk with you, brainstorm a little bit and get this off the ground for you.

Or, if you prefer:

- You can go to http://www.plumberseo.net/apply-now and enter your contact information and we'll get back to you and schedule the assessment and do our research.